MODERN WEAPONS
COMPARED AND CONTRASTED

ARTILLERY
AND
MISSILES

MARTIN J. DOUGHERTY

rosen publishing's
rosen
central®

New York

This edition first published in 2013 by:

The Rosen Publishing Group, Inc.
29 East 21st Street
New York, NY 10010

Additional end matter copyright © 2013 by The Rosen Publishing Group, Inc.

Library of Congress Cataloging-in-Publication Data

Dougherty, Martin J.
Artillery and missiles/Martin J. Dougherty.
     p. cm.—(Modern weapons: compared and contrasted)
Includes bibliographical references and index.
ISBN 978-1-4488-9247-1 (library binding)
1. Guided missiles. 2. Artillery. 3. Rockets (Ordnance) I. Title.
UG1310.D68 2013
623.4'1—dc23

2012034793

Manufactured in the United States of America

CPSIA Compliance Information: Batch #W13YA: For further information, contact Rosen Publishing, New York, New York, at 1-800-237-9932.

Copyright © 2012 by Amber Books Ltd. First published in 2012 by Amber Books Ltd.

Contents

Introduction

The function of artillery is to attack distant targets, usually by indirect fire with large quantities of explosives. Within this general concept there are several distinct roles, ranging from strategic nuclear strikes against targets on another continent to relatively short-range bombardment of enemy forces. Guided missiles may travel in a ballistic arc or fly like small aircraft, gaining the latter the name "cruise missiles." The addition of GPS guidance systems to many previously unguided rocket weapons has blurred the line between guided missiles and battlefield rocket systems.

Artillery weapons can be subdivided into two general types – rocket systems and "tube" artillery, i.e. weapons that launch an unpowered projectile from a barrel. Traditionally, tube artillery includes mortars (very short-barrelled weapons firing in a very high arc), howitzers (short-barrelled low-velocity weapons firing in a high arc) and guns (long-barrelled, high-velocity weapons firing in a shallower arc). However, these distinctions have become less sharp due to the introduction of weapons that do not fit into any clear category.

LEFT: A battery of British AS-90 self-propelled guns from the Royal Horse Artillery fire rounds in Basra, Iraq, 2008.

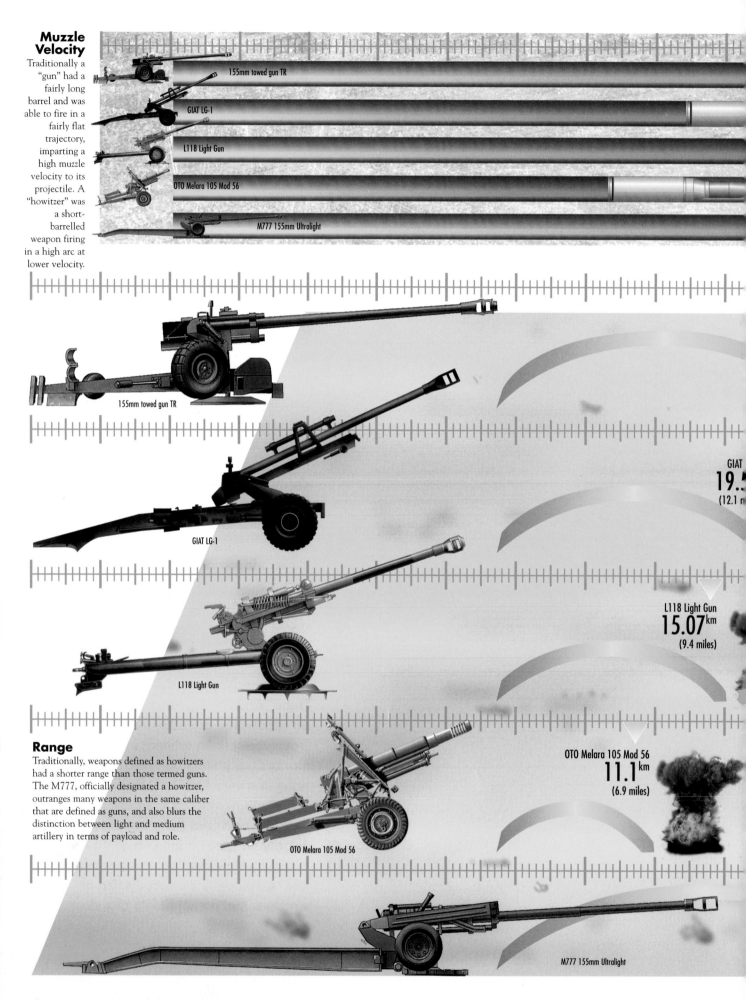

Muzzle Velocity

Traditionally a "gun" had a fairly long barrel and was able to fire in a fairly flat trajectory, imparting a high muzzle velocity to its projectile. A "howitzer" was a short-barrelled weapon firing in a high arc at lower velocity.

155mm towed gun TR

GIAT LG-1

L118 Light Gun

OTO Melara 105 Mod 56

M777 155mm Ultralight

155mm towed gun TR

GIAT LG-1

GIAT
19.5
(12.1 m

L118 Light Gun

L118 Light Gun
15.07km
(9.4 miles)

Range

Traditionally, weapons defined as howitzers had a shorter range than those termed guns. The M777, officially designated a howitzer, outranges many weapons in the same caliber that are defined as guns, and also blurs the distinction between light and medium artillery in terms of payload and role.

OTO Melara 105 Mod 56
11.1km
(6.9 miles)

OTO Melara 105 Mod 56

M777 155mm Ultralight

CHAPTER 1

Light and Medium Artillery

Range vs Muzzle Velocity

▶ **155mm towed gun TR**
▶ **GIAT LG-1**
▶ **L118 Light Gun**
▶ **OTO Melara 105 Mod 56**
▶ *M777 155mm Ultralight*

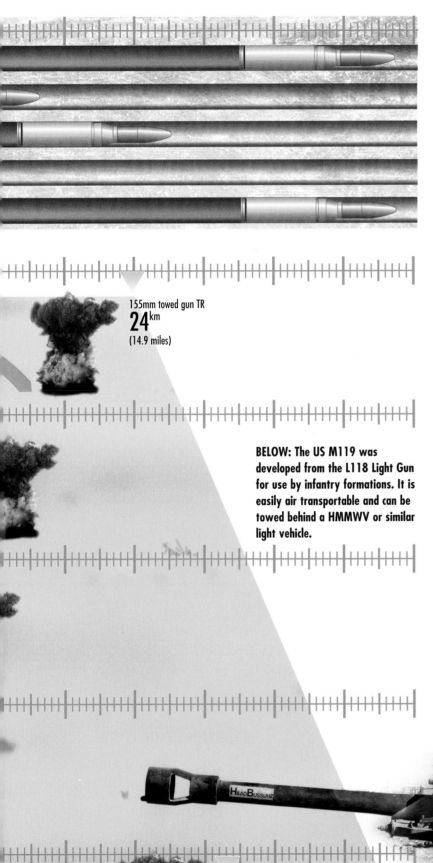

155mm towed gun TR
24km
(14.9 miles)

BELOW: The US M119 was developed from the L118 Light Gun for use by infantry formations. It is easily air transportable and can be towed behind a HMMWV or similar light vehicle.

M777 155mm Ultralight
40km
(24.9 miles)

Light artillery has the advantage of being relatively easy to move around. Guns can be transported by air or towed by light vehicles. However, this has traditionally limited the caliber and thus the hitting power of light-artillery weapons. A caliber of 105mm (4.1in) is standard, although recent developments in technology have allowed more powerful weapons to be fielded. These include the 155mm (6.1in) M777, which was designed from the outset to create a heavier-caliber weapon that could still operate within light-artillery parameters. Such weapons blur the line between light and medium artillery; by caliber they might be considered medium guns, but they can fulfill both the light and the medium roles.

The invention of weapons capable of performing both functions caused the term gun-howitzer to come into being, but it is more common to define a weapon as a gun or howitzer based on the preference of the designers. Thus the short-barrelled Oto Melara 105 is termed a howitzer, as is the long-barrelled M777. The L118 Light Gun, with the same muzzle velocity as the OTO Melara, is a gun, but the higher-velocity LG-1 is a howitzer. There seem no longer to be any hard-and-fast rules about designation.

CHAPTER 2

Heavy Artillery

Effective Range, Caliber and Elevation

▶ **Palmaria**
▶ **2S4 Tyulpan**
▶ **M110**
▶ **Primus 155mm**
▶ **2S7 Pion**

Many heavy artillery systems use very powerful weapons, with guns of 203mm (8in) or even greater caliber being common. However, "heavy artillery" is arguably a role rather than a class of weapons. Its function is to deliver as much indirect firepower as possible on the enemy at long range, usually against large or static targets such as troop concentrations or fortifications. If very heavy guns are not available, then the heavy artillery role falls on whatever weapons are there to be called on.

The US M110 and Russian 2S7 Pion are true self-propelled heavy artillery weapons, mounting 203mm (8in) guns. The lighter 155mm (6.1in) guns of the Primus and Palmaria weapons systems can serve a similar function at comparable ranges, but they deliver a smaller payload per shell and may not be effective against some targets. On the other hand, lighter weapons systems are more flexible; when not attempting to fill the heavy-artillery niche they can be quickly redeployed for other artillery tasks. The 2S4 Tyulpan mounts an extremely heavy (240mm/9.45in) weapon, which is defined as a breech-loading mortar rather than a gun. The barrel is short relative to the weapon's caliber, which greatly reduces the weapon's weight but also its effective range.

With advanced extended-range ammunition, the Tyulpan can rival some gun systems for range, but its normal projectiles have a range of only about 10km (6.2 miles). Extremely heavy, short-ranged weapons of this sort are primarily useful when attacking fortifications. In a fluid battle environment they will frequently be unable to get into range of the enemy.

RIGHT: A Cold War-era M110 SP gun takes part in exercises. Artillery gives a force the capability to strike at a distant enemy and to pound defensive positions into wreckage. It cannot capture an objective nor win battles alone, but artillery support can make the task facing other arms much easier.

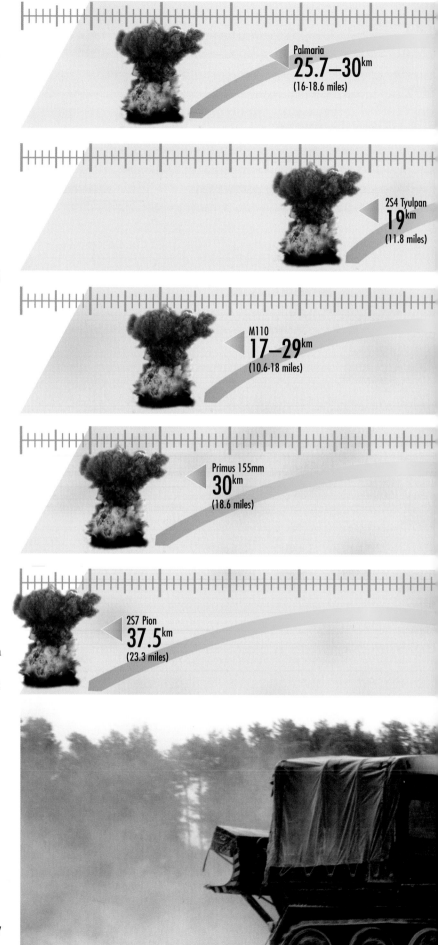

Palmaria
25.7–30km
(16-18.6 miles)

2S4 Tyulpan
19km
(11.8 miles)

M110
17–29km
(10.6-18 miles)

Primus 155mm
30km
(18.6 miles)

2S7 Pion
37.5km
(23.3 miles)

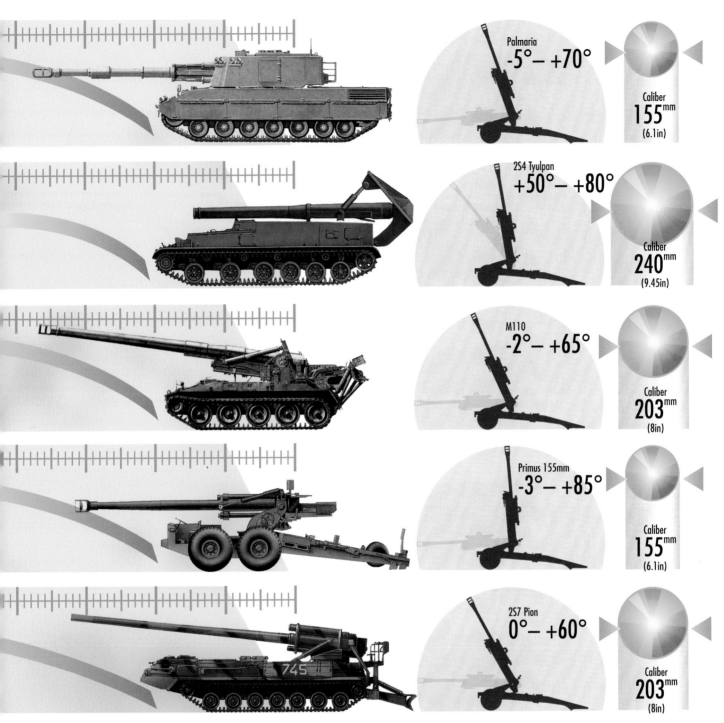

Palmaria

-5° – +70°

Caliber
155mm
(6.1in)

2S4 Tyulpan

+50° – +80°

Caliber
240mm
(9.45in)

M110

-2° – +65°

Caliber
203mm
(8in)

Primus 155mm

-3° – +85°

Caliber
155mm
(6.1in)

2S7 Pion

0° – +60°

Caliber
203mm
(8in)

Elevation and Caliber

An artillery shell (or any other projectile) will travel farthest when fired upward at a 45-degree angle. However, this may not be sufficient to clear obstructions. A greater elevation allows the shell to be lobbed over intervening objects and dropped almost vertically down into the target area, which negates much of the protection available to a dug-in enemy force.

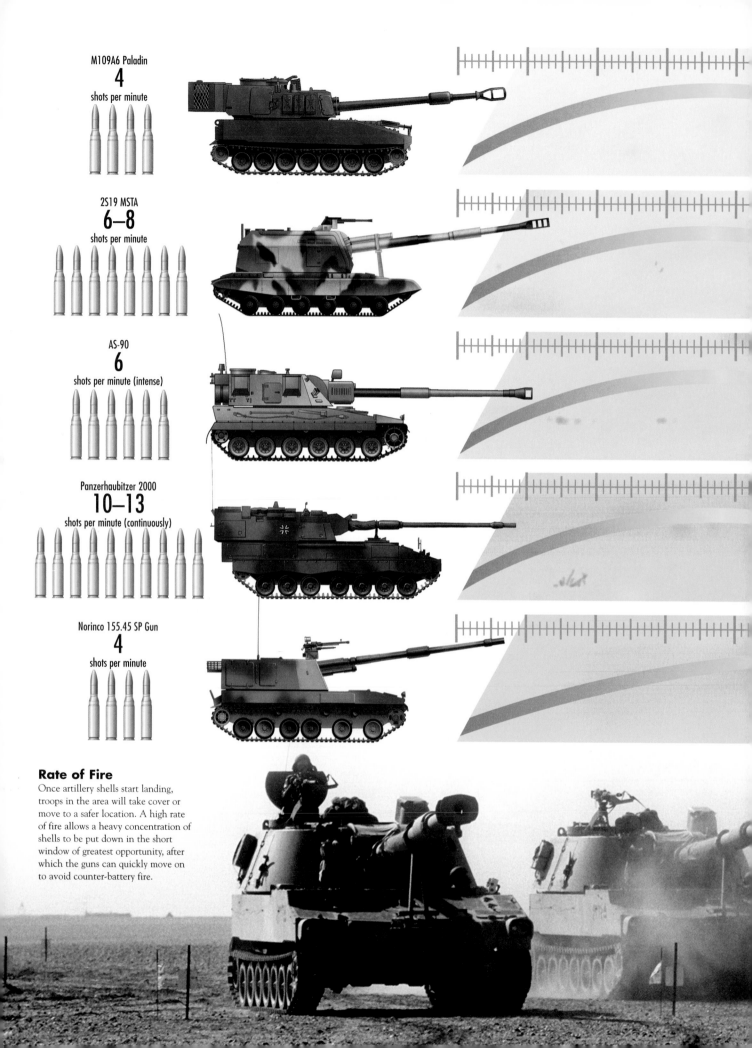

M109A6 Paladin

4

shots per minute

2S19 MSTA

6–8

shots per minute

AS-90

6

shots per minute (intense)

Panzerhaubitzer 2000

10–13

shots per minute (continuously)

Norinco 155.45 SP Gun

4

shots per minute

Rate of Fire

Once artillery shells start landing, troops in the area will take cover or move to a safer location. A high rate of fire allows a heavy concentration of shells to be put down in the short window of greatest opportunity, after which the guns can quickly move on to avoid counter-battery fire.

CHAPTER 3

Self-Propelled Guns 1

Effective Range and Rate of Fire

► **M109A6 Paladin**
► **2S19 MSTA**
► **AS-90**
► **Panzerhaubitzer 2000**
► **Norinco 155.45 SP Gun**

M109A6 Paladin Range
24–30km
(14.9-18.6 miles)

2S19 MSTA Range
29km
(18 miles)

AS-90 Range
30km
(18.6 miles)

Panzerhaubitzer 2000 Range
30km
(18.6 miles)

Norinco 155.45 SP Gun Range
39km
(24.2 miles)

Effective Range

Long-range fire capability allows the guns to remain safely behind friendly forces, and gives greater flexibility in terms of firing position. Shorter-range guns may have to shoot from predictable locations in order to hit a given target, and can offer support only to friendly formations in the nearby area. Long range increases the number of friendly units that the battery can support.

The "industry standard" for medium artillery is 155mm (6.1in) caliber, with a 39-caliber barrel being common. This means that the gun's length is 39 times its caliber, a size that experience has shown gives a good combination of range and mobility. The 39-caliber, 155mm (6.1in) gun was standardized by several NATO members in 1963, with the result that many artillery systems based on this agreement have very similar performance characteristics.

A longer gun would increase range, and some militaries have chosen to experiment with such weapons, typically using 52-caliber guns. Very long guns are prone to damage when moving rapidly cross-country. Self-propelled (SP) artillery is often called upon to do so, and even with a barrel support, the weight of the gun can be a problem. However, there are other ways to improve the range of artillery weapons, such as advanced munitions. Some of these use a rocket to boost the shell after launch, though this extra range comes at the price of a reduced warhead. Alternatively, the shell can be shaped to improve its aerodynamic performance, increasing range without altering the payload.

Most self-propelled artillery systems are capable of a high rate of fire for a short time. Even with autoloaders and power-assisted shell handling, there is a limit to how fast the gun can load and shoot at maximum intensity, and after a period of rapid fire the rate must be reduced. Thus artillery systems have a maximum rate of fire and a much slower sustained rate, which avoids excessive barrel overheating.

OPPOSITE: As with many SP guns, the barrel of the US M109A6 Paladin is clamped into a rest when travelling. This provides support and stability for the long gun, which might otherwise be damaged or distorted by the stresses of rapid cross-country movement.

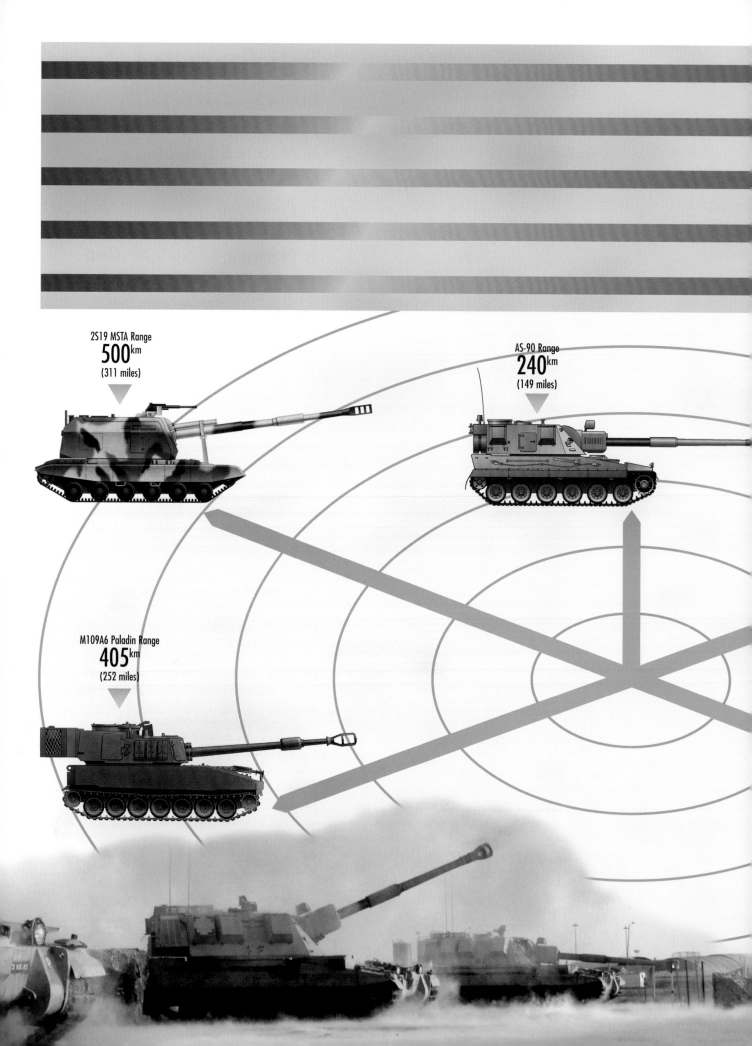

2S19 MSTA Range
500km
(311 miles)

AS-90 Range
240km
(149 miles)

M109A6 Paladin Range
405km
(252 miles)

CHAPTER 4

Self-Propelled Guns 2

Tactical Mobility: Speed and Road Range

▶ **M109A6 Paladin**

▶ **2S19 MSTA**

▶ **AS-90**

▶ **Panzerhaubitze 2000**

▶ **Norinco 155.45 SP Gun**

Norinco 155.45 SP Gun
56 km/h
(34.8mph)

Panzerhaubitze 2000
60 km/h
(37.3mph)

AS-90
55 km/h
(34.2mph)

2S19 MSTA
60 km/h
(37.3mph)

M109A6 Paladin
56 km/h
(34.8mph)

Speed

The speed of a self-propelled gun system is to some extent dictated by the forces it must support. The guns must be able to keep pace with armored or mechanized-infantry formations, while the ability to move faster than the tanks or infantry fighting vehicles is an advantage that will rarely be useful.

Panzerhaubitzer 2000 Range
420 km
(261 miles)

Road Range

The operational radius of SP guns varies considerably. It is acceptable for a gun system to require frequent refuelling, as it will rarely be in close proximity to the enemy and thus does not expose its support elements to enemy fire.

Norinco 155.45 SP Gun Range
450 km
(280 miles)

Self-propelled artillery first emerged during World War II, when the need was perceived for artillery that could keep pace with rapidly advancing tank formations. Early designs were crude, being little more than a field-artillery piece mounted on an obsolete tank chassis. Within a few years, the modern self-propelled gun began to emerge. Self-propelled artillery can go anywhere that a tank can. However, this does mean that self-propelled guns suffer from some of the same limitations. Tracked vehicles tend to be fuel-hungry and require a great deal of maintenance. This is less of a problem when they are integrated into an armored formation, as much of the necessary maintenance and repair capability is already in place.

Self-propelled guns are far more lightly armored than tanks, as in theory they are unlikely to encounter serious anti-tank weaponry. Their armor will usually protect their crew and systems from shell fragments, but more commonly the vehicles will avoid counter-battery fire by "shoot and scoot" tactics, firing several shots in rapid succession and then moving to a new position before the enemy can respond.

SP guns can be pushed into a close-support role, sometimes with great success. Any armored vehicle is a serious threat to an infantry force, and one armed with a very large gun can blast defenders out of their positions with ease.

During operations in Beirut in the 1980s, Israeli forces found it effective to create small battle groups of infantry supported by one tank and one self-propelled gun.

OPPOSITE: The British AS-90 was introduced in 1993 as a replacement for the 105mm Abbot self-propelled howitzer. Mounting the NATO compatible 155mm L31 gun, it is capable of firing three rounds in a 10-second burst, six rounds per minute for up to three minutes, or two rounds per minute for a duration of one hour.

CHAPTER 5

Wheeled SP Guns

Travel Range and Speed

▶ **G6**
▶ **Archer**
▶ **Caesar**
▶ **DANA**

Traditionally, self-propelled artillery systems were mounted on tracked chassis, often those of obsolete battle tanks. This not only gave the vehicle good cross-country mobility but also enabled it to absorb the recoil of a powerful gun. Recent developments in recoil-management technology have enabled a 155mm (6.1in) gun to be mounted on a wheeled chassis, whose off-road performance may be inferior to that of a track-laying vehicle but which can attain a higher speed over a longer distance on roads or reasonably level countryside.

Most wheeled self-propelled guns are built on a six-wheeled chassis, often one developed from off-road truck designs. Weight can be saved by dispensing with an armored turret, and instead mounting the gun over the vehicle hull. The crew areas and engine are still armored, and turretless vehicles are overall not significantly less well protected than more conventional equivalents. Most self-propelled artillery is lightly armored in any case, and defends itself best by avoiding contact with enemy forces.

While the Caesar and Archer systems use an open configuration, vehicles such as the DANA and G6 use a more conventional turret, housing the gun crew, loading mechanism and ammunition supply. The DANA was a ground-breaking design when it appeared in the 1970s; not only did it use a wheeled chassis but the weapon's autoloader was capable of operating even with the gun fully elevated. This feature was successful enough to become standard on later designs, and the DANA gun system has since evolved through several upgraded and export versions.

Travel Range

Wheeled gun systems offer up to twice the strategic mobility of an equivalent track-laying vehicle such as the M109A6 Paladin, but that is only part of the picture. Wheeled vehicles require less support in the field and are a good choice for forces needing to obtain more "tooth" than "tail" for their procurement dollars.

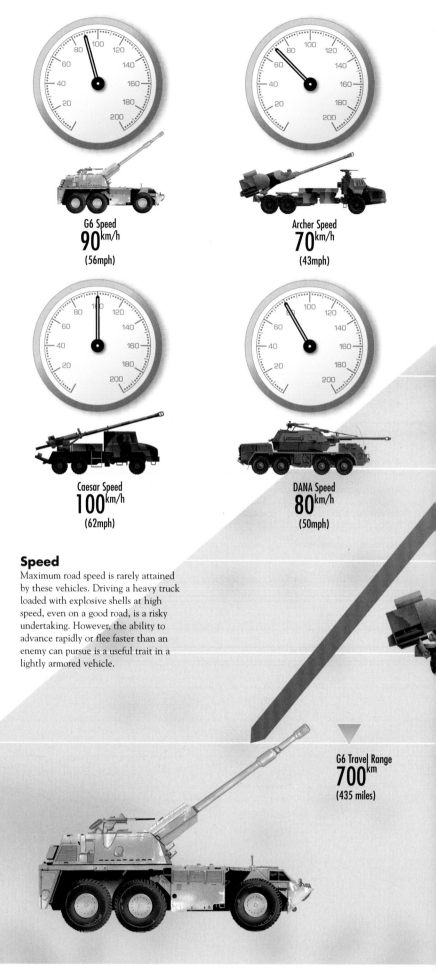

G6 Speed
90km/h
(56mph)

Archer Speed
70km/h
(43mph)

Caesar Speed
100km/h
(62mph)

DANA Speed
80km/h
(50mph)

Speed

Maximum road speed is rarely attained by these vehicles. Driving a heavy truck loaded with explosive shells at high speed, even on a good road, is a risky undertaking. However, the ability to advance rapidly or flee faster than an enemy can pursue is a useful trait in a lightly armored vehicle.

G6 Travel Range
700km
(435 miles)

1 A Swedish-made Archer takes part in exercises during winter. The system is fully automated, with a remote-controlled weapon station mounted on a modified 6x6 chassis of the Volvo A30D all-terrain articulated hauler.

Archer Travel Range
500^{km}
(311 miles)

Caesar Travel Range
600^{km}
(373 miles)

DANA Travel Range
600^{km}
(373 miles)

CHAPTER 6

Short- to Medium-Range Rocket Artillery Systems

Effective Range and Rate of Fire

▶ **BM-21 Grad**
▶ **TOS-1 MRL**
▶ **M77 Oganj MLRS**
▶ **ASTROS II**

The original artillery rockets were destructive but rather random, sometimes even turning back on their launchers. The invention of propellants that burn more evenly, along with a better understanding of aerodynamics, has enabled the artillery rocket to become a reliable support system in the modern era. Rocket systems are still less accurate than "tube" artillery – i.e. guns and howitzers – but they can achieve a good effective range and carry a powerful payload.

Rockets are launched in quick succession, so the vehicle can move soon after opening fire and thus avoid counter-battery fire. A gun could only deliver a couple of shells in the time that a rocket system can launch up to 40 rockets.

The inaccuracy of the rockets can sometimes be an advantage; a salvo launched at the same spot will spread out in flight and create a larger beaten zone. At shorter ranges, the salvo will remain concentrated and many warheads will hit a small area in a short period.

Effective Range

Rocket systems lack the range of tube artillery, and are less precise. Their primary role is in saturating a target area with warheads in a very short space of time. The two primary advantages of rocket systems are cheapness and the ability to dump a large payload onto a target in a few seconds. A rocket system can be built onto a fairly standard truck, as it does not have to absorb the recoil of a heavy gun, and can fire from any fairly level and firm surface without much preparation. This creates an inexpensive and easy-to-maintain artillery capability.

BM-21 Grad
20km
(12.4 miles)

M77 Oganj MLRS
20km
(12.4 miles)

ASTROS II
9–30km
(5.6-18.6 miles)

LEFT: A Saudi Arabian Avibras ASTROS II SS-30 rocket leaves its launch system, mounted on the back of a Tectran 6x6 AV-LMU truck, during Operation Desert Shield.

BM-21 Grad

TOS-1 MRL
3.5km
(2.2 miles)

TOS-1 MRL

M77 Oganj MLRS

ASTROS II

Rate of Fire

Once loaded, a rocket system can fire off all its ammunition in a period of just a few seconds. Reloading can be a lengthy process, however, so sustained fire rates are not very high.

BM-21 Salvo
2
rockets per sec

BM-21 Grad

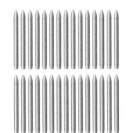

TOS-1 Salvo
30
rockets in 15 secs

TOS-1 MRL

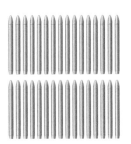

M77 Oganj Salvo
32
rockets in 20 secs

M77 Oganj MLRS

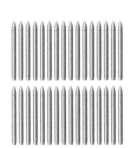

ASTROS II Salvo
32
rockets

ASTROS II

CHAPTER 7

Long-Range Rocket Artillery Systems

Effective Range and Rate of Fire

► **Type 89 MLRS**
► **BM-30 Smerch**
► **AR1A MLRS**
► **GMLRS**
► **HIMARS**

Rockets are not powered all the way to the target. They accelerate continuously until their fuel burns out, then follow a ballistic arc like any other projectile. A rocket is larger and has more wind resistance than a shell, and is far more prone to wind effects during its flight. Over short distances this may not be very significant, but traditionally long-range rocket systems have been notoriously inaccurate and primarily useful for harassing fire against "area" targets.

Modern rocket systems are assisted by ballistic computers that can take input from satellites, existing maps, and data sent from other combat formations to calculate the optimum firing solution. However, even if the system tries to take into account known wind conditions, wind is inherently variable and can still cause significant inaccuracy. One solution is to fit rockets with a GPS (Global Positioning System) guidance system, turning them into something between a traditional unguided rocket and a guided missile.

Using GPS is cheap compared with conventional missile guidance, as it relies on a satellite system that is already in place, but it is not as precise as a true missile-guidance system. GPS enables a rocket to guide itself to a position with reasonable accuracy, but there is no guarantee that the target will be there when it arrives. A GPS-guided rocket attacks a point on the ground; it is up to the user to determine if a suitable target will be present when the rocket gets there.

LEFT: The US M270 Multiple Launch Rocket System (MLRS) has been in service since the mid-1980s. A salvo of 12 rockets can saturate a one kilometer square (0.4-square-mile) area with bomblets, delivering ferocious firepower in an instant.

Effective Range

Achieving long range with a rocket system requires either reducing the payload to fit in more propellant, or increasing the rocket's overall size. At longer ranges a rocket salvo will disperse or may miss entirely, negating the main advantage of rocket artillery: the delivery of immense firepower in a short space of time.

Type 89 MLRS Range
30^{km}
(18.6 miles)

BM-30 Smerch Range
70^{km}
(43 miles)

AR1A MLRS Range
130^{km}
(81 miles)

GMLRS range
60^{km}
(37 miles)

HIMARS Range
32^{km}
(19.9 miles)

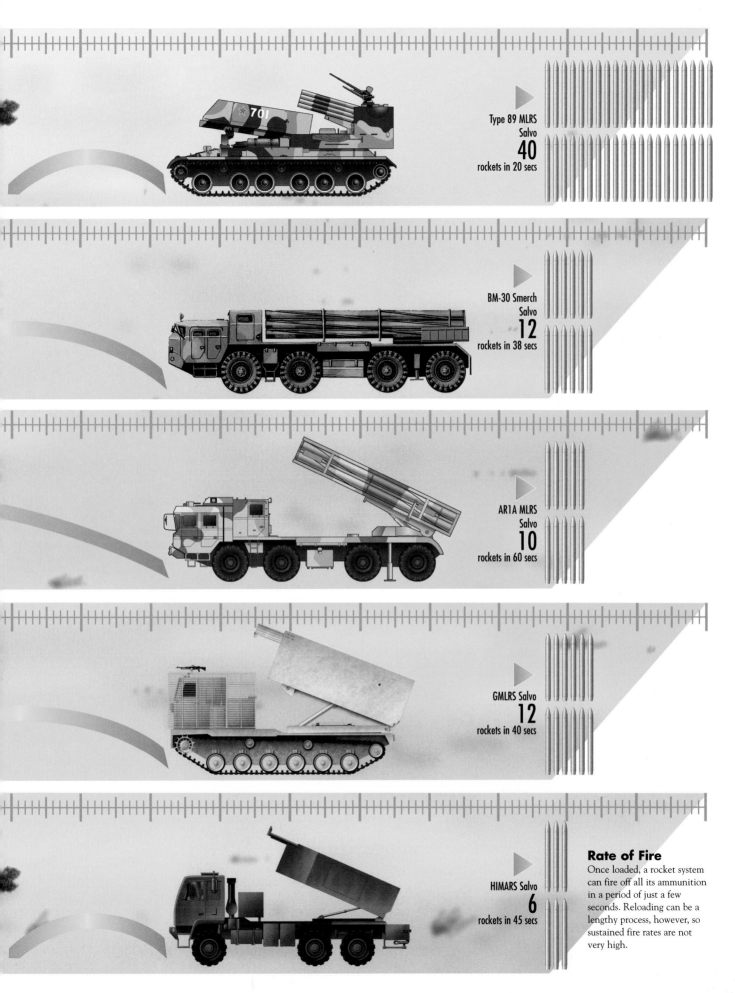

Type 89 MLRS
Salvo
40
rockets in 20 secs

BM-30 Smerch
Salvo
12
rockets in 38 secs

AR1A MLRS
Salvo
10
rockets in 60 secs

GMLRS Salvo
12
rockets in 40 secs

HIMARS Salvo
6
rockets in 45 secs

Rate of Fire
Once loaded, a rocket system can fire off all its ammunition in a period of just a few seconds. Reloading can be a lengthy process, however, so sustained fire rates are not very high.

CHAPTER 8

Anti-Aircraft Artillery

Effective Range and Rate of Fire

▶ **PGZ95 SPAAA**
▶ **Sidam 25**
▶ **9K22 Tunguska**
▶ **Type 87 SPAAG**

The need for mobile anti-aircraft weaponry that could move with an armored formation was demonstrated during World War II. At the same time the practice of using obsolete armored-vehicle chassis as platforms for anti-aircraft artillery (AAA) was established. Although AAA units are not intended to come into direct contact with the enemy's ground forces, nothing is guaranteed in warfare.

Although missiles have proved their worth in the anti-aircraft role, especially against distant or fast-moving threats, there is still a place for guns. For close-range air defense against fixed-wing aircraft, especially helicopters, rapid-fire gun systems can be highly effective.

Hybrid gun/missile systems offer a range of options, though these come at the price of increased cost and complexity. Missiles are used for area defense, engaging any aircraft that ventures within their reach, with the guns as a backup for use against close-range targets. The primary advantage of pure gun systems is cheapness, allowing more potential targets to be protected for the same amount of budget dollars.

Effective Range

The effective range of a gun-based anti-aircraft system is fairly short compared with that of a missile. Unguided projectiles take time to reach their target at longer range and the point of aim cannot be corrected once they are fired, greatly increasing the chances of a miss.

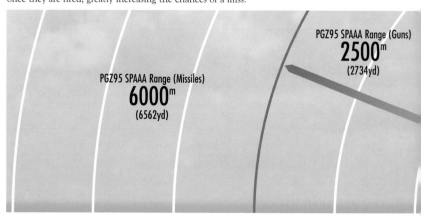

PGZ95 SPAAA Range (Guns)
2500m
(2734yd)

PGZ95 SPAAA Range (Missiles)
6000m
(6562yd)

BELOW: A Russian 9K22 Tunguska parades through Moscow. Modern air-defense vehicles must be able to track and engage targets as diverse as fast-moving strike jets, low, slow helicopters and possibly small reconnaissance drones or even enemy missiles. A gun system may have a secondary use as a high-firepower ground-combat asset.

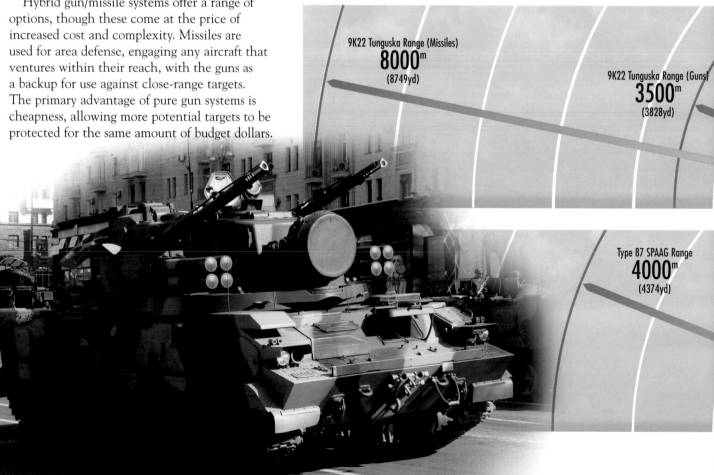

9K22 Tunguska Range (Missiles)
8000m
(8749yd)

9K22 Tunguska Range (Guns)
3500m
(3828yd)

Type 87 SPAAG Range
4000m
(4374yd)

Rate of Fire

In order to hit and damage a fast-moving target, AAA systems attempt to throw what amounts to a wall of projectiles in the path of the aircraft. The more rounds are passing through the same volume of air as the target, the greater the chances of a hit.

Sidam 25 Range
2000^m
(2187yd)

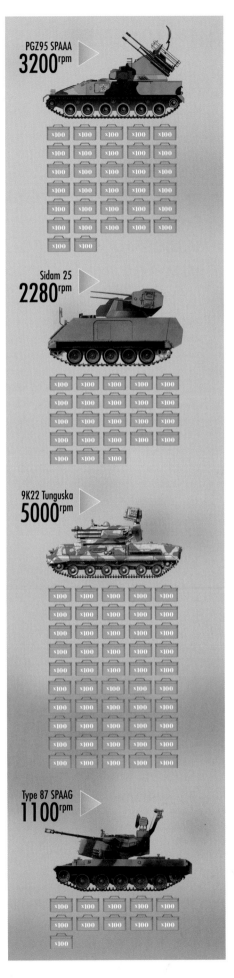

PGZ95 SPAAA
3200rpm

Sidam 25
2280rpm

9K22 Tunguska
5000rpm

Type 87 SPAAG
1100rpm

CHAPTER 9

Air-Defense Missile Launchers

Effective Range and Ceiling

▶ **ADATS**
▶ **2K12 KUB (SA-6 "Gainful")**
▶ **Crotale Mk 3**
▶ **S-300PMU (SA-10 "Grumble")**
▶ **MIM-104 Patriot**

Two of the critical factors for an air-defense missile are its range and ceiling. Ceiling is the maximum height at which an interception is possible. Light, man-portable air-defense missiles have a low ceiling and are primarily useful against helicopters or low-flying ground-attack aircraft. Weapons of this sort can be used to defend a point target but are ineffective against high-flying aircraft, whether they are attacking or simply flying over on their way to another target.

Longer-range missiles can be used for area defense, intercepting enemy aircraft at higher altitudes and greater distances. This can allow a launcher to cover a greater radius, or permit a missile to chase down an aircraft that attempts to flee out of range. A long-range missile system can dominate local airspace and make air operations in the area extremely hazardous. Ironically, perhaps, this makes it a high-priority target for enemy air forces, requiring that the heavy launchers be protected by shorter-range weapons.

In order to achieve long range and a high intercept ceiling, a large and expensive missile is needed, and this must be partnered with a suitable launcher. Thus most militaries field a mix of air-defense weapons, with a few powerful, long-range systems for area defense and a greater number of short-range missiles to protect specific targets. Close-in defense is often supplemented by rapid-fire guns. The US-designed ADATS (Air Defense Anti-Tank) missile system is unusual, in that it is designed to launch the same missiles against aircraft or ground targets. Its range is short, but a warhead capable of crippling a tank will leave little of an aircraft it hits.

Effective Range

Attack aircraft often carry standoff missiles, and can defeat many short-range air-defense systems by launching their weapons from beyond the system's engagement range, and then retiring. Longer-range systems can cover a larger area and intercept intruders earlier.

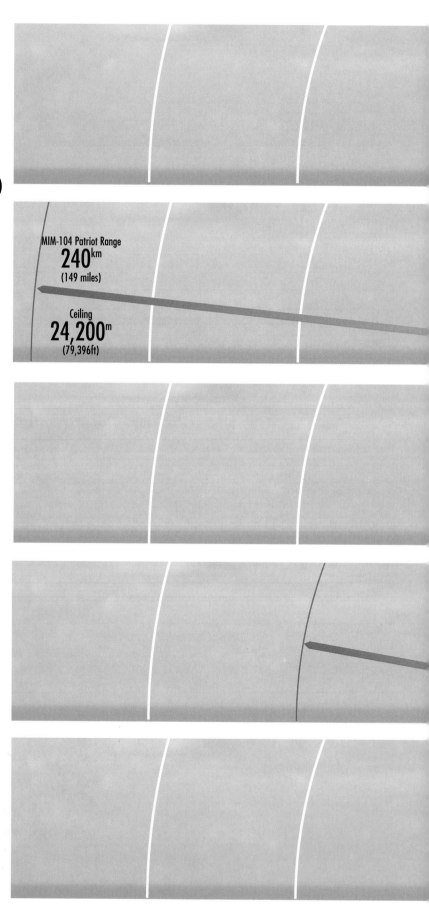

MIM-104 Patriot Range
240km
(149 miles)

Ceiling
24,200m
(79,396ft)

Ceiling

The largest air-defense missiles can intercept a high-flying bomber or even a short-range ballistic missile. Decades ago it was possible to defeat air defenses by simply flying above their engagement envelope. Today, a low-level, high-speed penetration offers a better chance of success.

ADATS

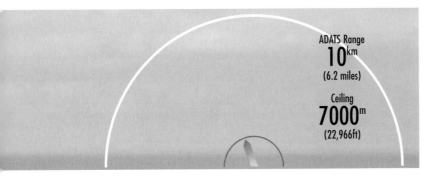

ADATS Range
10km
(6.2 miles)

Ceiling
7000m
(22,966ft)

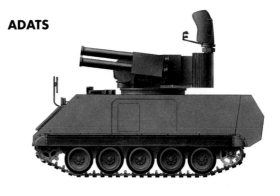

MIM-104 Patriot

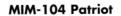

Crotale Mk 3

Crotale Mk 3 Range
16km
(9.9 miles)

Ceiling
9000m
(29,528ft)

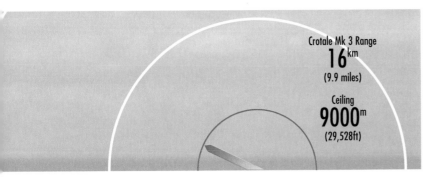

S-300PMU

S-300PMU Range
150km
(93 miles)

Ceiling
25,000m
(82,021ft)

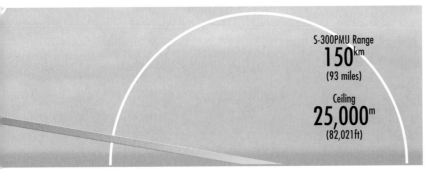

2K12 KUB

2K12 KUB Range
20km
(12.4 miles)

Ceiling
7000m
(22,966ft)

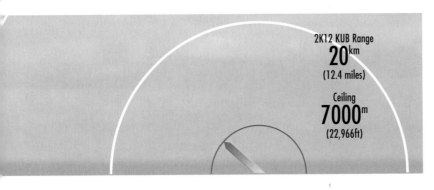

CHAPTER 10

Standoff Missiles

Effective Range and Warhead Weight

▶ **AGM-86C CALCM**
▶ **AGM-154 JSOW**
▶ **Hsiung Feng II**
▶ **Storm Shadow**
▶ **AGM-129 ACM**

A cruise missile is, in many ways, a small automated aircraft that can travel autonomously to its target area before making an attack. During this "cruise" part of the mission, guidance may be provided by an inertial or GPS system, or by terrain-matching. This compares radar data with known terrain features and allows the missile to find its way to a programmed destination. Some missiles use inertial and GPS guidance for the terminal attack phase; others have a thermal-imaging system.

Many cruise missiles are air launched, allowing a standoff strike without exposing the launch platform to enemy air defenses. The small, low-flying missile is better able to penetrate a defended area than an aircraft, and many cruise missiles are designed to be "stealthy," making them difficult to detect or target. Other designs can be deployed on ground launchers or naval vessels; in many cases there are variants of the same missile that can be launched from different platforms.

The US AGM-86 CALCM (Conventional Air-Launched Cruise Missile) was developed from a nuclear-armed weapon to meet changing operational requirements. It permitted the B-52 strategic bomber to become a launch platform for precise non-nuclear strikes.

Warhead Types

Most cruise missiles can carry various warheads, including cluster bombs or penetrator warheads intended to punch deep into a bunker before exploding. This mission requires great precision. Storm Shadow achieves it by using a thermal camera in its nose. At the start of the attack phase, the missile gains altitude and then dives, enabling the camera to seek the target from above.

AGM-86C CALCM

AGM-154 JSOW

Hsiung Feng II

Storm Shadow

AGM-129 ACM

BELOW: Cruise missiles can be carried aboard mobile container-launchers, which can shift position to avoid attack.

The range of a standoff missile depends on its role. Smaller examples, such as the AGM-154 JSOW (Joint Standoff Weapon), are unpowered and are effectively long-range glide bombs. Larger weapons such as Hsiung Feng are more like aircraft in their own right.

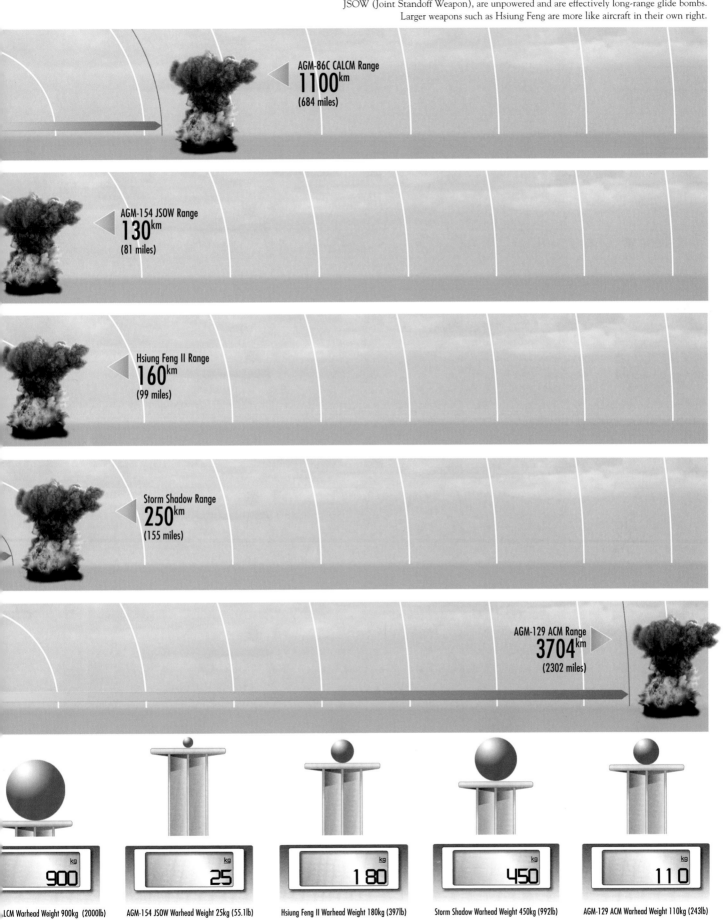

AGM-86C CALCM Range
1100km
(684 miles)

AGM-154 JSOW Range
130km
(81 miles)

Hsiung Feng II Range
160km
(99 miles)

Storm Shadow Range
250km
(155 miles)

AGM-129 ACM Range
3704km
(2302 miles)

kg
900

kg
25

kg
180

kg
450

kg
110

LCM Warhead Weight 900kg (2000lb)

AGM-154 JSOW Warhead Weight 25kg (55.1lb)

Hsiung Feng II Warhead Weight 180kg (397lb)

Storm Shadow Warhead Weight 450kg (992lb)

AGM-129 ACM Warhead Weight 110kg (243lb)

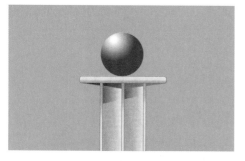

AGM-84H SLAM-ER Warhead Weight 221kg (487lb)

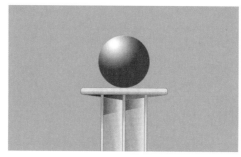

Kh-59MK (AS-18 "Kazoo") Warhead Weight 320kg (705lb)

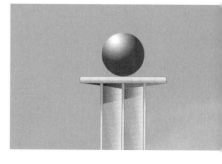

AGM-130 Warhead Weight 240kg (529lb)

Warhead Weight

The warhead is often a relatively small part of the weight of the missile, although its size determines the magnitude of impact the missile will have.

AGM-84H SLAM-ER
Length
3800mm
(149.6in)

Kh-59MK
(AS-18 "Kazoo")
Length
5700mm
(224.4in)

AGM-130
Length
3920mm
(154.3in)

AGM-84H SLAM-ER Launch Weight 691kg (1523lb)

Kh-59MK (AS-18 "Kazoo") Launch Weight 930kg (2050lb)

AGM-130 Launch Weight 1323kg (2917lb)

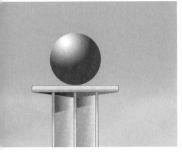

GBU-67 Zoobin Warhead Weight 340kg (750lb)

Brimstone Warhead weight not known

CHAPTER 11

Modern Tactical Air-to-Surface Missiles 1

Warhead Weight, Launch Weight and Length

- ▶ **AGM-84H SLAM-ER**
- ▶ **Kh-59MK (AS-18 "Kazoo")**
- ▶ **AGM-130**
- ▶ **GBU-67 Zoobin**
- ▶ **Brimstone**

Hitting a ground target from a fast-moving platform such as an aircraft is a challenge at the best of times. Even with a good ballistic computer, "dumb" bombs are extremely inaccurate. Bombs also require the attacking aircraft to fly over the target, which may be heavily defended. Guided missiles offer both greater precision and the ability to launch the weapon at a distance from the target. This "standoff" capability increases survivability for attack aircraft.

A bomb can be mostly payload, but a missile needs to give up space for propellant, guidance fins and its targeting system. This reduces the size of payload that a missile of a given size can carry. The proportions of payload to overall missile weight vary considerably, but as a rule, if long range is desired, then this can only come at the expense of payload, or else a bigger missile will have to be constructed. This remains an option, but there is a limit to how big a missile can get and still be carried by a typical strike aircraft.

By way of comparison, a Mk 83 bomb, often referred to as a 500kg or 1000lb bomb although its exact weight can vary, carries a 200kg (441lb) warhead in a package about 3000mm (118.1in) long. The 430kg (948lb) warhead of a Mk 84 bomb (925kg/2039lb total weight) is carried in a casing 3280mm (129.1in) long. Bombs do offer more "bang per kilo/pound" than missiles, which may be important when considering the load an aircraft can carry, but this must be balanced against standoff-attack capability and precision.

67 Zoobin
th
80mm
.2in)

ZOOBIN

Brimstone
Length
1800mm
(70.9in)

Launch Weight

Air-launched weapons tend to be designed to fit existing aircraft capabilities. The weapon's performance must be balanced against the capability of strike aircraft to carry it, forcing weapon designs into several rough categories determined by previous generations of weaponry.

GBU-67 Zoobin Launch Weight 560kg (1235lb)

Brimstone Launch Weight 48.5kg (107lb)

Chapter 12

Modern Tactical Air-to-Surface Missiles 2

Effective Range

- ▶ **AGM-84H SLAM-ER**
- ▶ **Kh-59MK (AS-18 "Kazoo")**
- ▶ **AGM-130**
- ▶ **GBU-67 Zoobin**
- ▶ **Brimstone**

The addition of guidance systems to freefall ordnance (i.e. bombs) has created a new role for unpowered munitions, somewhere between a traditional bomb and a missile. A bomb normally falls away from under an aircraft, accelerating downward while retaining much of the launching platform's airspeed. This seriously limits the range of a bomb, unless it is dropped from a great height. In the past, high-altitude bombing led to low accuracy, but the advent of guidance systems negated this problem.

A bomb can be given increased range by "tossing" it. Instead of flying straight and level to drop its bombs, the aircraft pulls up sharply at high speed, launching the bomb in a high arc, which extends its range significantly. The bomb's guidance system can, however, only alter its flight path from side to side, or shorten its flight. An unpowered bomb cannot glide or extend its range in the way that a missile can.

Thus, missiles offer greater flexibility than guided bombs. A missile can accelerate or gain height in order to reach a distant target, and in some cases can be given a re-attack capability. A missile with this function can turn around and have another try if it misses its target. Thrust can also be useful if the target is moving and in the case of missiles that can be retargeted in flight. A missile can change its aim point to anywhere within its maximum range and will often arrive at the target area at higher speed than a bomb, making defensive fire problematic.

RIGHT: Carrying one air-to-surface missile on each of its underwing pylons, a single aircraft can make standoff strikes against several high-value targets in the course of a single mission. A similar number of attacks with short-range weapons might pose an unacceptable level of risk to the aircraft and its pilot.

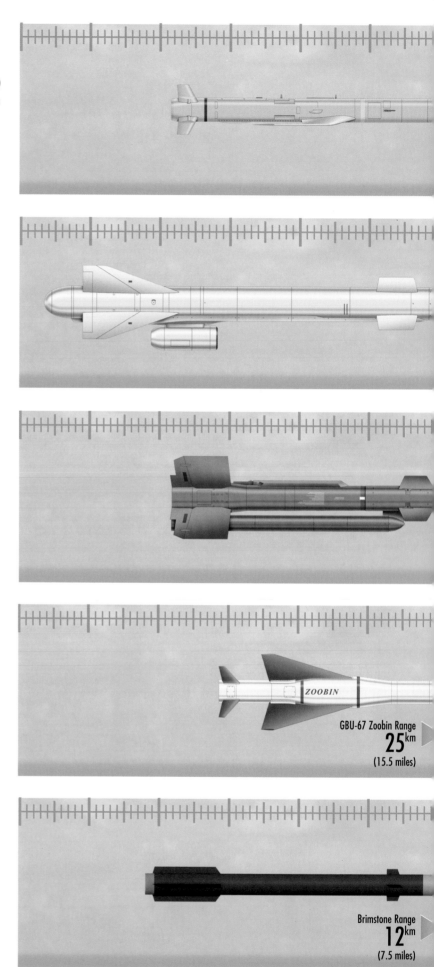

GBU-67 Zoobin Range
25^{km}
(15.5 miles)

Brimstone Range
12^{km}
(7.5 miles)

Range
Longer-range missiles are, in general, larger and more expensive than short-range weapons. They must carry guidance systems for the approach to the target area as well as for the final attack, and often require larger and more sophisticated launch platforms.

AGM-84H SLAM-ER Range
124km
(77 miles)

Kh-59MK (AS-18 "Kazoo") Range
200km
(124 miles)

AGM-130 Range
60km
(37 miles)

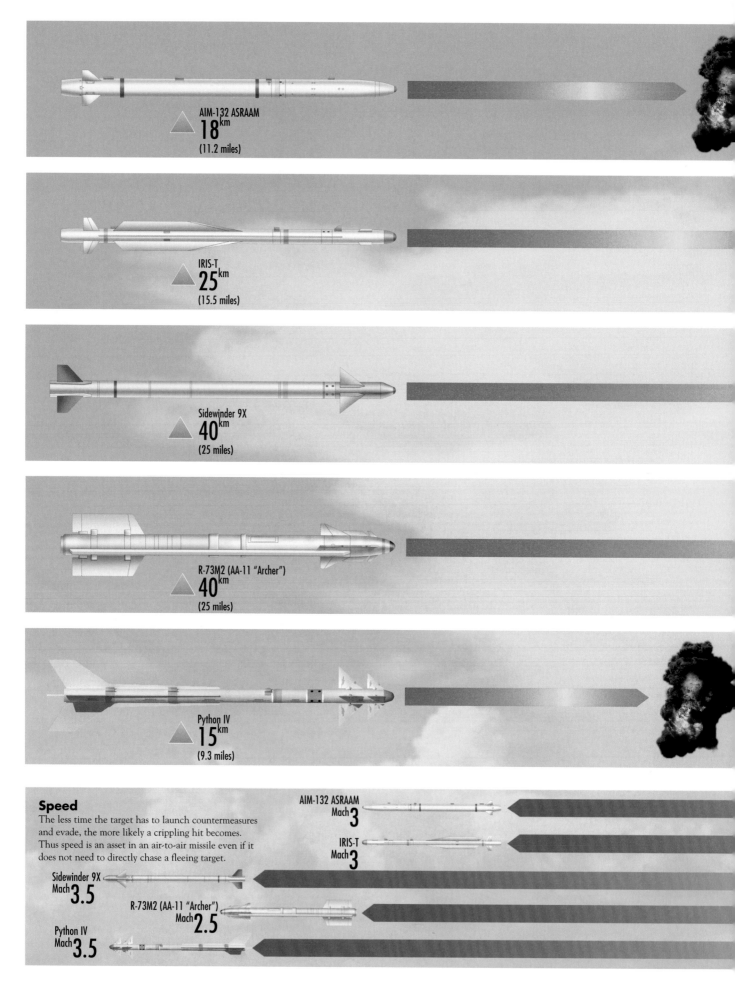

AIM-132 ASRAAM
18^{km}
(11.2 miles)

IRIS-T
25^{km}
(15.5 miles)

Sidewinder 9X
40^{km}
(25 miles)

R-73M2 (AA-11 "Archer")
40^{km}
(25 miles)

Python IV
15^{km}
(9.3 miles)

Speed
The less time the target has to launch countermeasures and evade, the more likely a crippling hit becomes. Thus speed is an asset in an air-to-air missile even if it does not need to directly chase a fleeing target.

AIM-132 ASRAAM
Mach **3**

IRIS-T
Mach **3**

Sidewinder 9X
Mach **3.5**

R-73M2 (AA-11 "Archer")
Mach **2.5**

Python IV
Mach **3.5**

CHAPTER 13

Air-to-Air Missiles

Effective Range and Speed

▶ **AIM-132 ASRAAM**
▶ **IRIS-T**
▶ **Sidewinder 9X**
▶ **R-73M2 (AA-11 "Archer")**
▶ **Python IV**

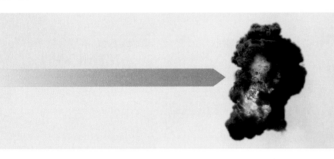

Long-range air-to-air missiles are normally guided by radar, and may be fired at a target that is too distant to see. Shorter-range missiles, sometimes referred to as "dogfight" missiles, generally use infrared homing. Early infrared seekers were rather primitive and would lock onto the largest heat source in their arc of vision. This was sometimes the sun, and even if the missile locked onto the hot engine exhaust of an enemy aircraft it could easily be distracted by flares dropped as a countermeasure.

Modern heat-seeking missiles are much less likely to be distracted by other heat sources, but can still be confused by flares dropped by the target aircraft. A combination of flares and well-timed evasive maneuvers can cause a missile to overshoot its intended target. However, a missile does not necessarily need to make a direct hit. A contact explosion is highly destructive, but missiles are fused to explode in proximity to the target if a hit is not obtained. This creates a shower of missile fragments that can inflict crippling damage on an enemy aircraft.

A new generation of missiles is emerging that can lock onto a target that is not in front of the launching aircraft. By means of a targeting system fitted to the pilot's helmet, a missile can be locked onto any target the pilot can see, swerving violently after launch to begin its pursuit. An attack on a target outside the normal arc is known as an "over the shoulder launch."

Effective Range

Long-range missiles give the user a massive advantage in air-to-air combat, as they can down some of the enemy force before they get close enough to launch their own weapons.

BELOW: A Eurofighter Typhoon fires an MBDA ASRAAM (Advanced Short-Range Air-to-Air Missile) during target practice.

CHAPTER 14

Air-Launched Anti-Tank Missiles

Effective Range and Length

▶ **AGM-114K Hellfire II**
▶ **Brimstone**
▶ **Nimrod**
▶ **Mokopa**

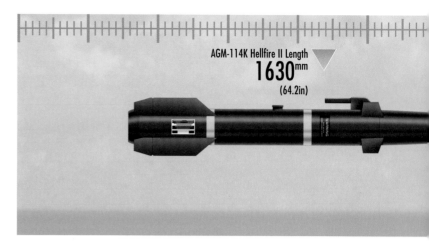

AGM-114K Hellfire II Length
1630mm
(64.2in)

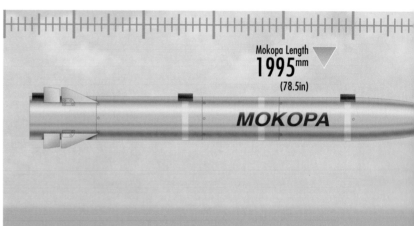

Mokopa Length
1995mm
(78.5in)

MOKOPA

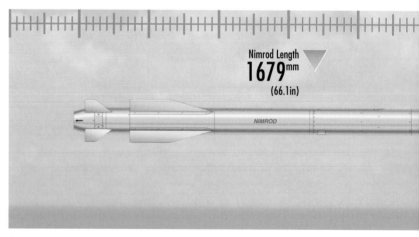

Nimrod Length
1679mm
(66.1in)

NIMROD

Brimstone Length
1800mm
(70.9in)

MBDA BRIMSTONE

During World War II, all manner of aircraft were converted to the "tank-buster" role, including some that were highly inappropriate, such as large bombers. Tank busters of the era attacked at low altitude, flying relatively slowly compared with today's strike jets, and although some used cannon, most delivered their attack with rockets. From these inaccurate but nevertheless effective weapons were developed a new generation of guided anti-armor weapons, which permit a fast-moving aircraft to destroy a single enemy tank with great precision.

The Hellfire missile was designed from the outset to be usable by both fixed-wing aircraft and helicopters. Most early Hellfire models were laser-guided, with some using radar guidance. The ability to receive guidance from other sources than the launching platform allowed a missile strike to be delivered and the aircraft to leave the vicinity or seek cover behind terrain while a designator on the ground or aboard a helicopter took over control of the missiles.

Hellfire set the standard for many following missiles. The Nimrod was designed to be used by CH-53 assault helicopters. The South African Mokopa missile was developed largely due to an international arms embargo that prevented imports, while Brimstone started out as a developed version of Hellfire. Brimstone initially used radar guidance, but operational experience showed that a "man in the loop" was often necessary. A dual-mode variant was introduced, which can use autonomous radar guidance or semi-active laser homing. The latter requires manual targeting using a laser designator, allowing the missile to be precision guided.

Although developed as anti-tank weapons, many missiles have matured into multi-role precision systems, capable of carrying a range of payloads for use against bunkers, ships and personnel concentrations.

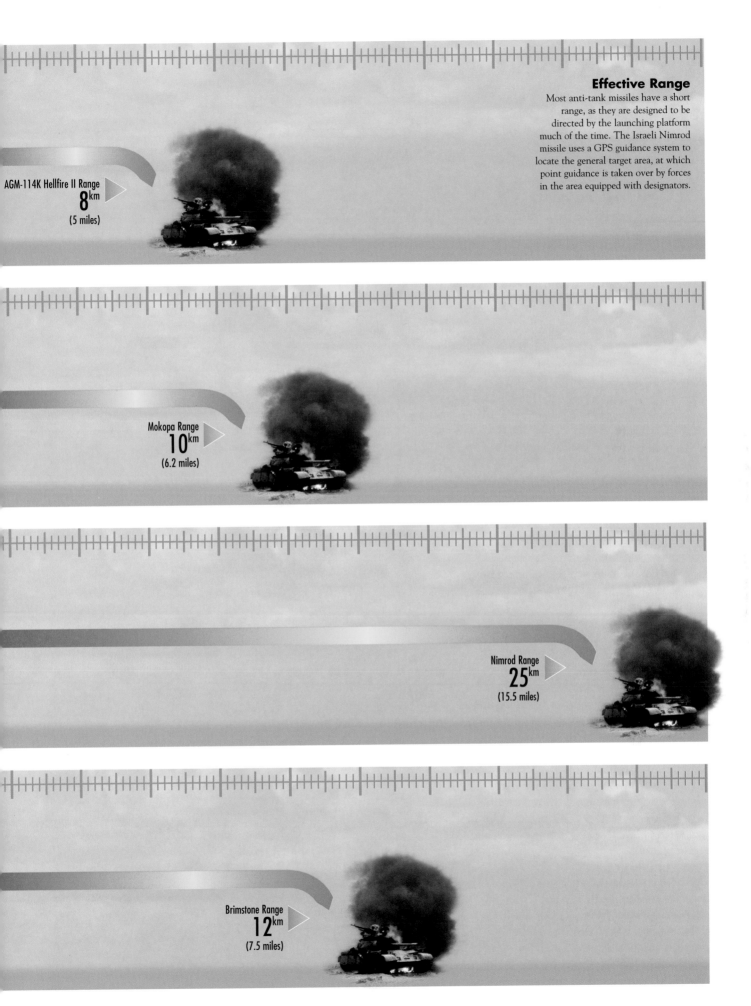

Effective Range

Most anti-tank missiles have a short range, as they are designed to be directed by the launching platform much of the time. The Israeli Nimrod missile uses a GPS guidance system to locate the general target area, at which point guidance is taken over by forces in the area equipped with designators.

AGM-114K Hellfire II Range
8km
(5 miles)

Mokopa Range
10km
(6.2 miles)

Nimrod Range
25km
(15.5 miles)

Brimstone Range
12km
(7.5 miles)

CHAPTER 15
Anti-Tank Guided Weapons Systems

Effective Range and Weight

▶ **FGM-148 Javelin**
▶ **Spike-MR**
▶ **Raytheon Griffin**

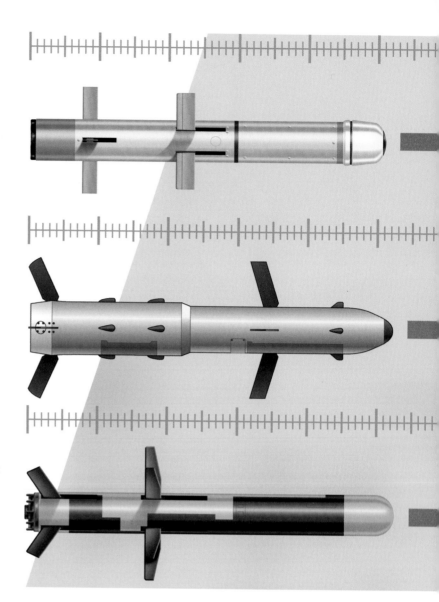

The ability to destroy tanks, or at least to pose a threat to them, is one of the most important capabilities a military force can possess. It has been suggested that "if you can't fight tanks, you can't fight," which underlines the importance of having an anti-armor capability within infantry forces. In the past, it was sufficient to provide rocket-propelled grenades and disposable unguided weapons, but modern advanced main battle tanks (MBTs) are too well armored to be seriously damaged by such weapons, though they remain useful against lighter vehicles and targets such as bunkers.

The new generation of guided anti-tank weapons allows infantry to attack armored vehicles from a greater distance with a good chance of a hit, and in many cases these weapons can be switched to a different target while the missile is in flight. The guidance systems of missiles such as Javelin and Spike permit top-attack mode to be selected. The armor of a tank or other combat vehicle tends to be weakest on top. Wherever possible, this is the preferred mode of attack.

The increasing levels of protection provided to armored vehicles has necessitated a gradual expansion in warhead size since the introduction of the first light anti-armor weapons. There is a limit to how large and powerful a warhead can be and remain man-portable, so warhead technology has also had to advance. Some missiles use tandem warheads, which make two attacks on the same spot in rapid succession, as a countermeasure against reactive armor.

RIGHT: The Javelin missile system uses a "soft launch" to avoid injuring the operator. A short-duration rocket motor drives the missile out of the tube, after which it coasts for a short distance before the main motor ignites. This greatly reduces backblast, though it is still unsafe to be directly behind the launcher.

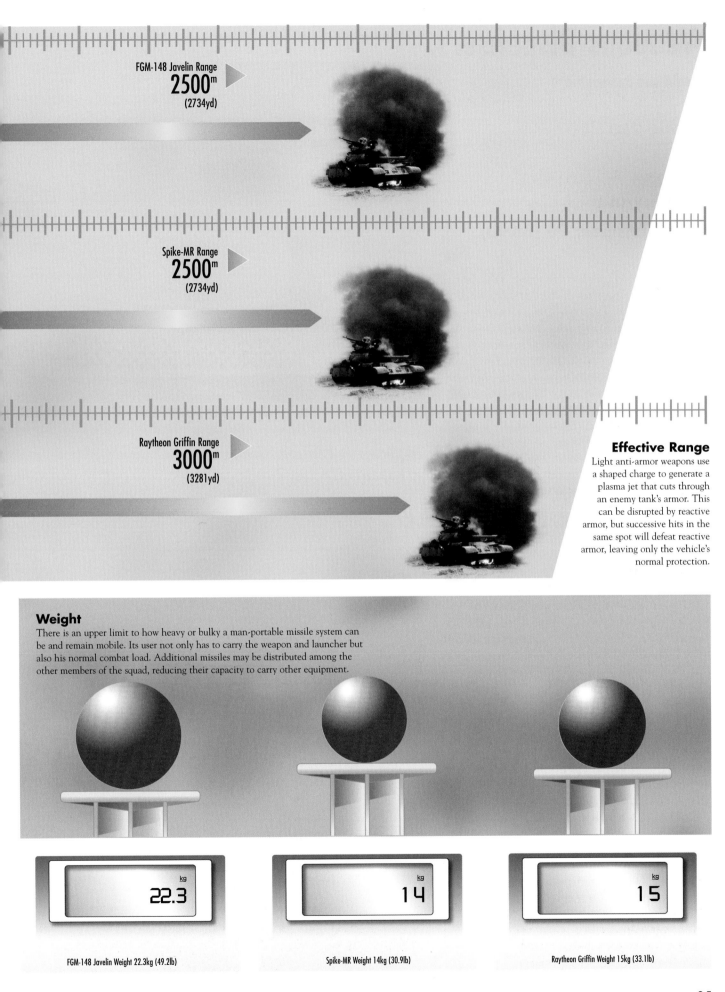

FGM-148 Javelin Range
2500^m
(2734yd)

Spike-MR Range
2500^m
(2734yd)

Raytheon Griffin Range
3000^m
(3281yd)

Effective Range

Light anti-armor weapons use a shaped charge to generate a plasma jet that cuts through an enemy tank's armor. This can be disrupted by reactive armor, but successive hits in the same spot will defeat reactive armor, leaving only the vehicle's normal protection.

Weight

There is an upper limit to how heavy or bulky a man-portable missile system can be and remain mobile. Its user not only has to carry the weapon and launcher but also his normal combat load. Additional missiles may be distributed among the other members of the squad, reducing their capacity to carry other equipment.

22.3 kg

14 kg

15 kg

FGM-148 Javelin Weight 22.3kg (49.2lb)

Spike-MR Weight 14kg (30.9lb)

Raytheon Griffin Weight 15kg (33.1lb)

CHAPTER 16

Weapons Dispensers

Weight and Submunitions

▶ **RBK-250**
▶ **Kite**
▶ **JP233**
▶ **CBU-100 Rockeye**
▶ **Bombkapsel 90 (BK90)**

Submunition dispensers are simply vehicles that carry a large number of smaller weapons to the target area. Many are air-dropped, and they are often constructed to the same dimensions as a conventional bomb. The payload is normally anti-personnel bomblets, or cluster bombs, but it can also include anti-tank munitions, mines or more exotic payloads such as anti-electrical bomblets designed to damage power-transmission stations. Specialist submunitions also potentially include chemical weapons or propaganda leaflets, and runway-denial systems. The latter often incorporate both direct-attack munitions and delayed-detonation mines to make clearance and repair more difficult.

The purpose of using submunitions rather than a single warhead is to saturate the target area, which has caused some controversy, as cluster munitions are regarded as indiscriminate weapons in some quarters. While it is true that everyone and everything in the target area is attacked by exploding bomblets, the same is true for any weapon with a blast radius, such as conventional bombs, missiles and artillery shells. Cluster munitions simply do the same job more efficiently, over a wider area.

Cluster munitions can be delivered with great precision to a target area, but once there they are designed to saturate the area with great lethality. A near miss with a bomb or shell may be survivable, but the hail of fragments caused by anti-personnel bomblets has so much overlap that unprotected personnel are unlikely to escape.

The dispenser itself may be unguided or may incorporate various forms of guidance, including inertial, GPS or laser designation. This permits the payload to be delivered with great accuracy, though, as already noted, the submunitions will then be scattered so as to give maximum coverage of the target area. Weapons of this sort cannot be used for pinpoint attacks, but are extremely effective against area targets such as concentrations of vehicles or troops.

Submunitions

Submunitions vary in size. Anti-personnel bomblets can be very small, while anti-armor submunitions must pack a larger punch. The intensity of coverage depends on how many submunitions are carried and how widely they are scattered.

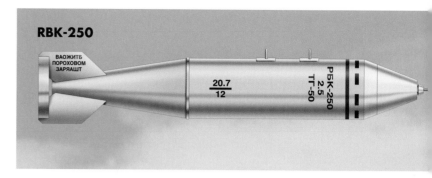

RBK-250

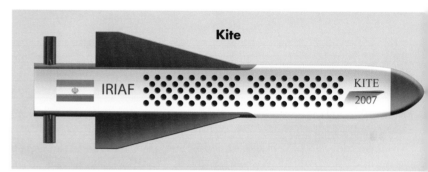

Kite

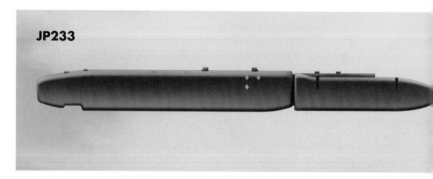

JP233

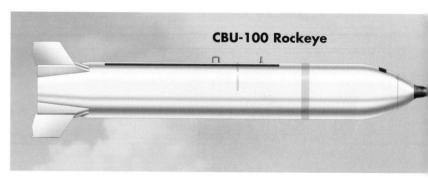

CBU-100 Rockeye

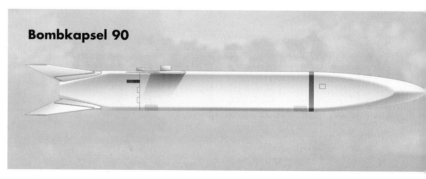

Bombkapsel 90

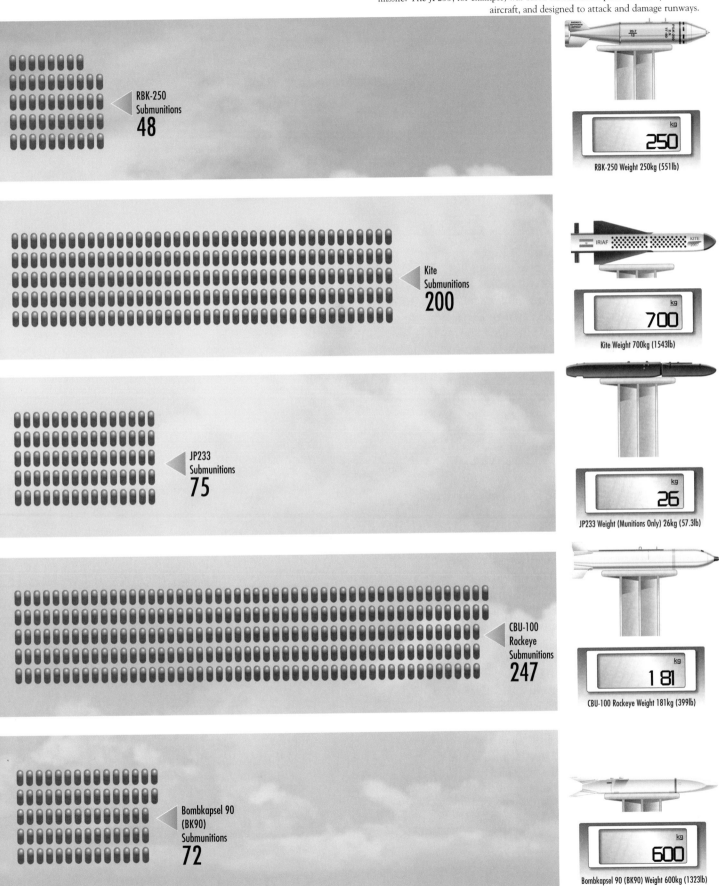

Weight

Submunition dispensers vary considerably in size and weight. Those intended to be deployed from aircraft normally correspond to the dimensions of an existing bomb or missile. The JP233, for example, was based on container pods carried by Tornado aircraft, and designed to attack and damage runways.

RBK-250
Submunitions
48

kg
250

RBK-250 Weight 250kg (551lb)

Kite
Submunitions
200

kg
700

Kite Weight 700kg (1543lb)

JP233
Submunitions
75

kg
26

JP233 Weight (Munitions Only) 26kg (57.3lb)

CBU-100
Rockeye
Submunitions
247

kg
181

CBU-100 Rockeye Weight 181kg (399lb)

Bombkapsel 90
(BK90)
Submunitions
72

kg
600

Bombkapsel 90 (BK90) Weight 600kg (1323lb)

CHAPTER 17

Bombs

Payload

- ▶ **Mk 82**
- ▶ **Mk 83**
- ▶ **Mk 84**
- ▶ **FAB-1500**

Unguided or "dumb" bombs are, at best, highly inaccurate. Precision can be improved by delivering the bombs at a very low level, but this action can pose a hazard to the launching aircraft. For this reason, retarded bombs were developed, which deploy air brakes after being dropped. These slow the bomb and allow the aircraft to clear the blast area. Unguided bombs can also be converted into guided weapons by fitting a GPS guidance kit, creating weapons that lack the precision of laser-guided bombs but that are still far more accurate than unguided equivalents.

The basic bomb in all these cases is much the same: an aerodynamic casing carrying as large a warhead as possible. The United States uses three standard sizes of bomb, designated Mk 82, Mk 83 and Mk 84, modelled on the traditional 500lb (227kg), 1000lb (454kg) and 2000lb (907kg) bombs. Decisions about what mix of bombs is most likely to be effective on a given mission must be based on the nature of the target and the delivery platform – some aircraft cannot carry the heavier bombs on their pylons.

Standard bomb payloads have remained more or less the same since World War II, when extensive experience was gained of the trade-off between bomb weight and effectiveness. A larger, single warhead is more effective against a point target like a bunker, but a pattern of smaller bombs will cause more destruction to a supply dump or troop concentration.

The Russian equivalent to the US Mk 80 series is designated FAB (from the Russian for "General Purpose Bomb"). These weapons, too, come in standard sizes modelled on traditional bomb payloads. Equivalents to the Mk 82, Mk 83 and Mk 84 all exist and can be delivered by tactical aircraft; there are also much more powerful FAB-1500 (1500kg/3307lb) and FAB-3000 (3000kg/6614lb) bombs, which can only be delivered by heavy bombers.

1 US Air Force ground crew load up M117 bombs under the wings of a B-52H long-range bomber.

FAB-1500
1500kg
(3307lb) ▶

Payload

Conventional general-purpose bombs offer a lot of "bang for the buck" as they give up little mass for guidance or propulsion systems, and thus can carry a proportionally larger warhead than a missile of the same nominal weight.

Weight 1500kg (3307lb)

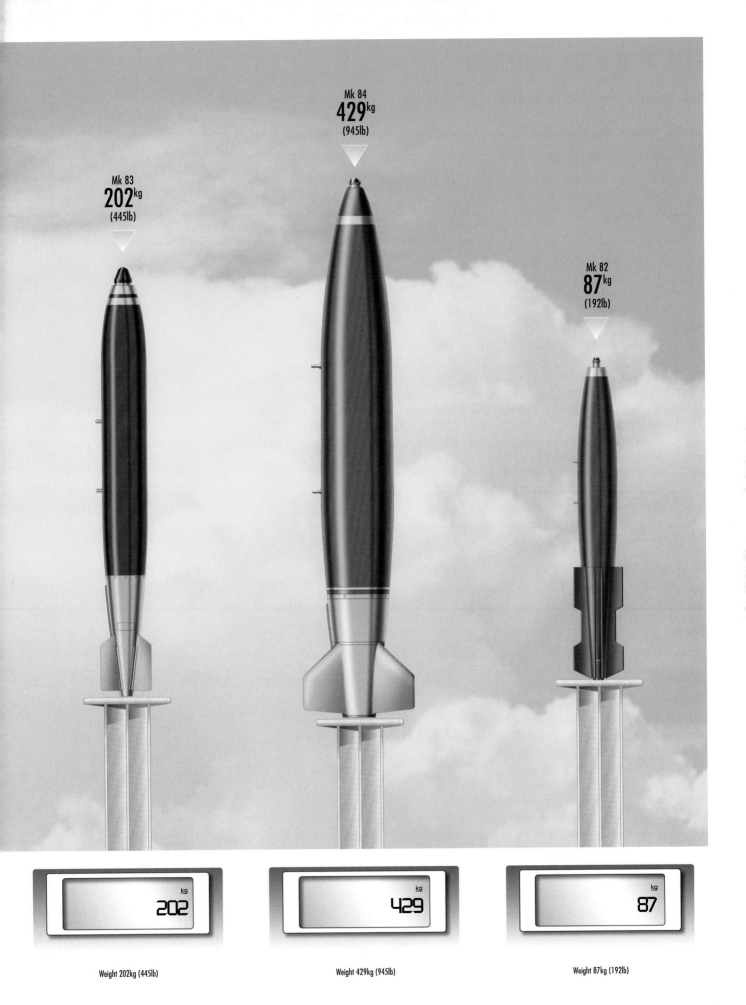

Mk 83
202kg
(445lb)

Mk 84
429kg
(945lb)

Mk 82
87kg
(192lb)

Weight 202kg (445lb)

Weight 429kg (945lb)

Weight 87kg (192lb)

CHAPTER 18

US Nuclear Bombs

Approximate Blast Radius of Effect

▶ **B57**

▶ **B61**

▶ **B83**

In addition to an electromagnetic pulse (EMP), which can disrupt communications and electronic equipment over a wide area, a nuclear explosion creates a massive amount of thermal (infrared) radiation, which will incinerate nearby personnel and objects, and start fires over a wider area. The flash may cause temporary blindness in anyone looking at it, and the detonation also emits a surge of ionizing radiation, which may irradiate the immediate surroundings.

The fireball will destroy anything within its radius and create a crater as well as sending a high-pressure wave of air (blast) outward. This is powerful enough to flatten nearby structures and will cause damage over a wide area. Air rushing back into the low-pressure area created by the blast causes secondary damage and also brings in dust that is then thrown upward to create the characteristic "mushroom cloud." This dust, which includes radioactive material and irradiated debris, then settles as "fallout" wherever the wind carries it.

The area over which these effects take place depends upon the yield of the weapon, rated in kilotons. One kiloton equates to 1016 tonnes (1000 tons) of TNT. The US B61 nuclear bomb is a variable-yield weapon, which can be set to deliver a given intensity of blast depending on the chosen target. The B61 can be delivered by a variety of aircraft, including the Lockheed Martin F-35 Lightning II. Its maximum yield is 340 kilotons for the "strategic" role, and can be set as low as 0.3 kilotons for "tactical" targets. By comparison, the B57 bomb was designed as a series of fixed-yield warheads ranging from 5 to 20 kilotons. The B83 is the largest US nuclear weapon and has a variable yield, with a maximum of 1.2 megatons.

RIGHT: The total destruction radius created by a nuclear weapon is perhaps smaller than many people might imagine, but this is only one of the weapon's effects. Near the impact or burst point, absolutely nothing will survive.

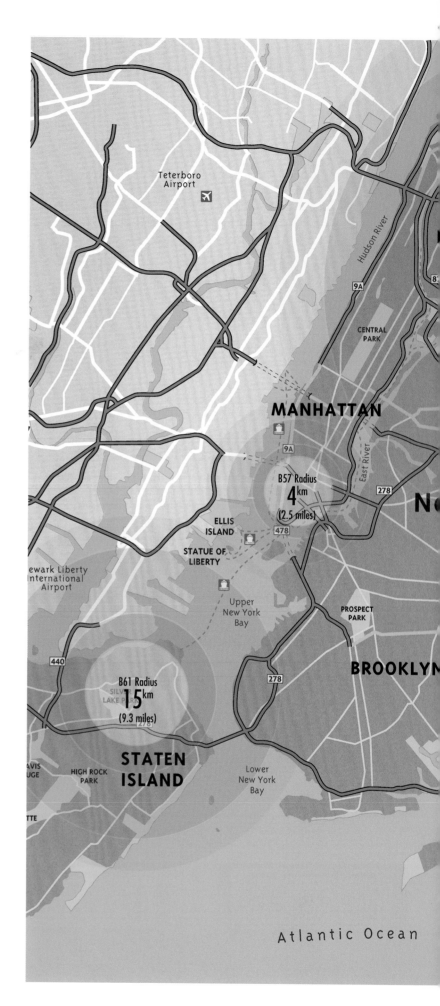

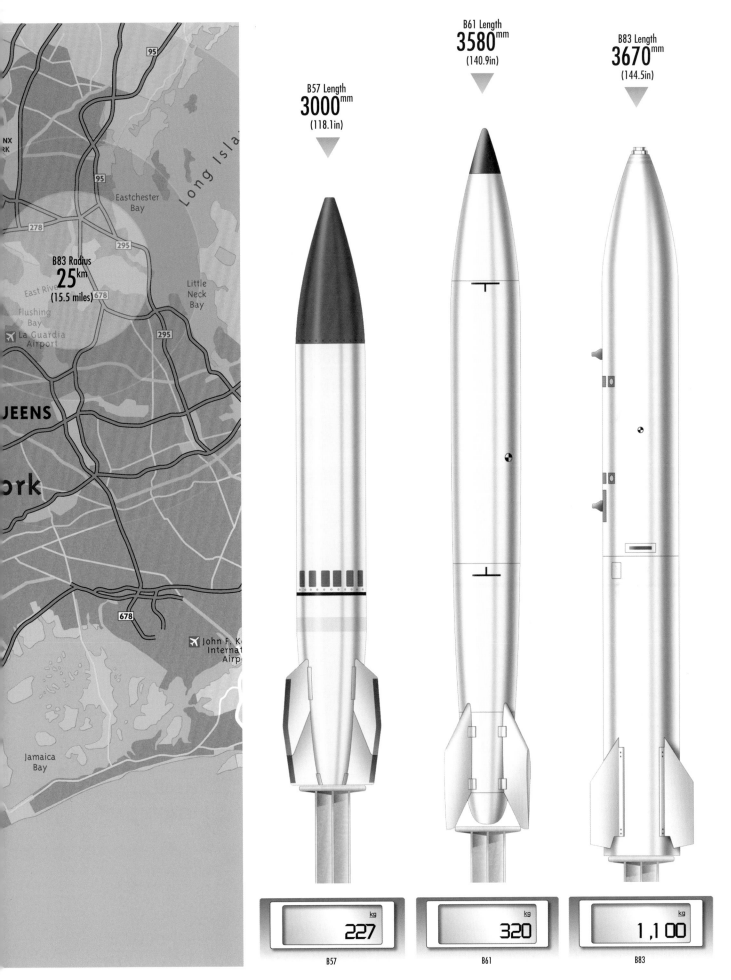

B57 Length
3000mm
(118.1in)

B61 Length
3580mm
(140.9in)

B83 Length
3670mm
(144.5in)

B83 Radius
25km
(15.5 miles)

kg
227

kg
320

kg
1,100

B57

B61

B83

CHAPTER 19

Nuclear Explosion: Number of Kilotons

Fallout Range

▶ **0.1 Kiloton**
▶ **1 Kiloton**
▶ **10 Kiloton**

The precise effects of a nuclear detonation depend on its location. A high-altitude (above 30km/18.6 miles) detonation does not produce a mushroom cloud or radioactive fallout. The fireball will not touch the ground, but direct radiation effects may be considerable. High-altitude bursts would normally be used to produce an electromagnetic pulse (EMP) and thereby damage electronic equipment. A lower air burst will cause mainly blast and thermal effects, and is more hazardous to people than structures.

A subsurface burst, where the warhead penetrates the ground before exploding, will cause heavy radioactive contamination of the area and very severe local effects, but smaller secondary effects. When a weapon is detonated on or close to the ground, local blast and thermal effects will be severe, and fallout will be considerable due to contaminated debris drawn up into the mushroom cloud. The diagram shows the effects of various warhead detonations within a major urban area.

Within the severe damage zone (red), few structures will remain intact and personnel casualties will be almost total. The area will also be heavily contaminated. Within the moderate damage zone (orange), strongly built structures (e.g. concrete) may survive more or less intact, but lighter buildings will be destroyed or heavily damaged. Personnel casualties are likely to be high, due to both the weapon's effects and secondary causes such as fires and collapsing buildings. Within the light damage zone (yellow), windows will be broken and buildings will suffer light structural damage. Damage patterns will be varied, as blast can rebound and be funnelled by structures. Immediate casualties are unlikely to be severe and will mostly be from secondary causes.

RIGHT: Damage zones are not clear-cut and may be patchy due to terrain and weather effects. Nearer to the point of detonation (Ground Zero), damage becomes more uniform and more severe until, close to Ground Zero, destruction becomes total.

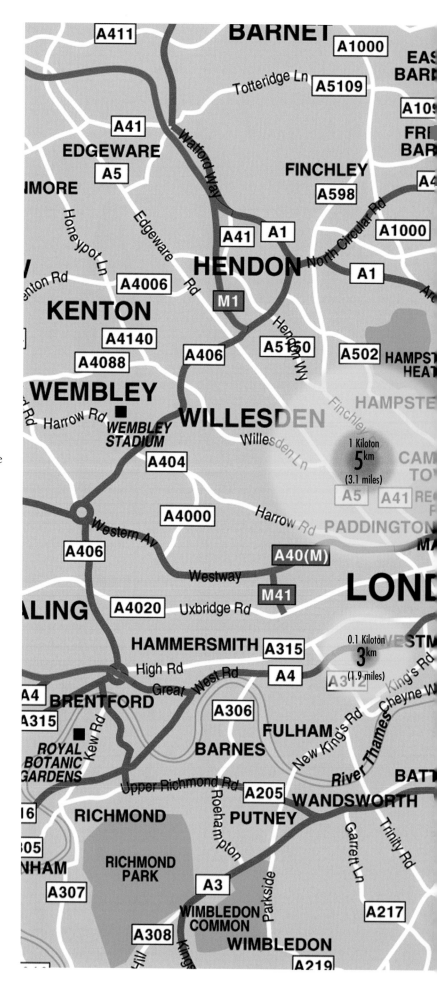

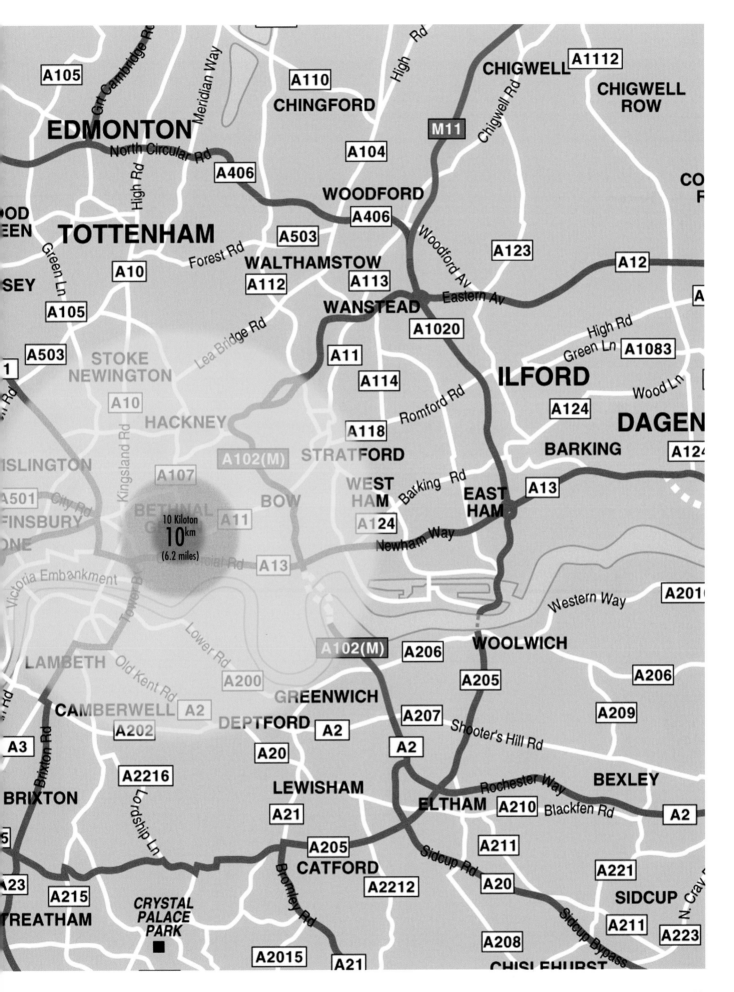

A105

A110

CHIGWELL

A1112

CHINGFORD

CHIGWELL ROW

M11

Chigwell Rd

EDMONTON

North Circular Rd

A104

A406

WOODFORD

A406

Meridian Way

High Rd

Woodford Av

A123

A12

TOTTENHAM

A503

Forest Rd

WALTHAMSTOW

Eastern Av

A10

A112

A113

High Rd

Green Ln

A1083

A105

Lea Bridge Rd

WANSTEAD

A1020

ILFORD

Green Ln

A503

STOKE NEWINGTON

A11

Wood Ln

1

A10

A114

Romford Rd

A124

DAGEN

Kingsland Rd

HACKNEY

A118

BARKING

ISLINGTON

A102(M)

STRATFORD

A124

A501

A107

WEST HAM

Barking Rd

EAST HAM

A13

FINSBURY

City Rd

BETHNAL G

A11

BOW

A124

A13

ONE

10 Kiloton
10km
(6.2 miles)

Newham Way

Victoria Embankment

ial Rd

A13

Lower Rd

Western Way

A201

LAMBETH

Old Kent Rd

A102(M)

A206

WOOLWICH

A206

A200

A205

CAMBERWELL

A2

GREENWICH

A207

A209

A202

DEPTFORD

A2

Shooter's Hill Rd

A3

A20

A2

BEXLEY

Brixton Rd

A2216

LEWISHAM

Rochester Way

A210

Blackfen Rd

A2

BRIXTON

Lordship Ln

A21

ELTHAM

A205

A211

A221

23

A205

CATFORD

Sidcup Rd

SIDCUP

A215

CRYSTAL PALACE PARK

A2212

A20

A211

A223

REATHAM

A2015

A21

A208

Sidcup Bypass

CHISLEHURST

43

Moscow

New York

CSS-4
12,900km
(8016 miles)

LGM-30G
13,000km
(8077 miles)

SS-18
16,000km
(9942 miles)

CHAPTER 20

Intercontinental Ballistic Missiles

Range

▶ **LGM-30G (United States)**
▶ **SS-18 (Russia)**
▶ **CSS-4 (China)**
▶ **Shahab-3 (Iran)**
▶ **Taepodong-1 (North Korea)**

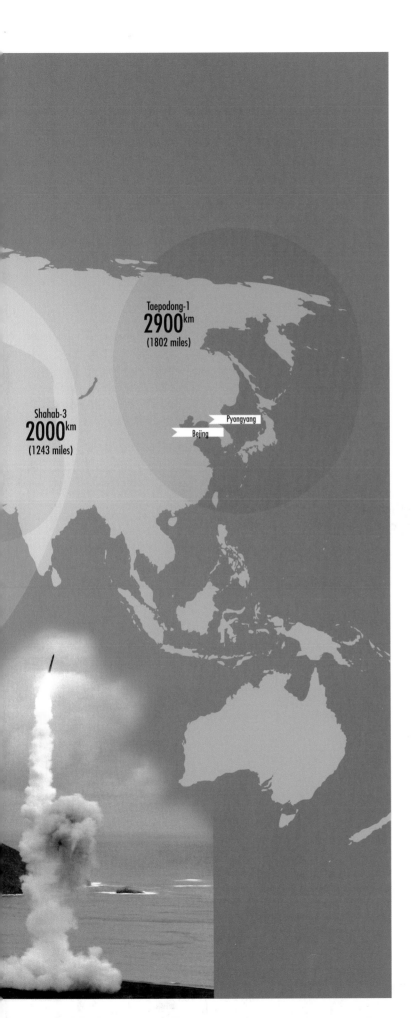

Taepodong-1
2900km
(1802 miles)

Shahab-3
2000km
(1243 miles)

Pyongyang

Bejing

Early nuclear bombs were sufficiently large and heavy that they could only be delivered by strategic bombers, and this required that the bombers penetrate deep into enemy airspace and then make a hazardous return flight after their attack. The invention of air-launched cruise missiles increased the survivability of the nuclear-bomber force, and therefore also the chance that weapons would actually reach their targets. However, it was the ballistic missile that made reliable delivery of nuclear weapons possible, and thus greatly increased the credibility of a deterrence policy. A ballistic missile is extremely hard to intercept, and can cover the distance between launcher and target in a fraction of the time required to fly there in a bomber. Missile accuracy has steadily increased over time, but this is only important when attacking very hard targets such as missile silos. Against population centers and industrial areas, a near miss with a nuclear warhead is every bit as effective as a direct hit.

Theater ballistic missiles are intended to be able to attack any target within their "theater of war," defined as within 3500km (2175 miles) of the launch point. The term has replaced earlier ones such as medium-range ballistic missile or intermediate-range ballistic missile. The longest-ranged missiles, those capable of attacking targets on another continent, are extremely large, expensive and difficult to develop, and are termed intercontinental ballistic missiles (ICBMs). Some nations protect their missile launch capabilities with hardened bunkers, while others use submarines to hide their weapons in the world's oceans.

LEFT: A Minuteman III missile takes off from somewhere on US soil. The LGM-30G Minuteman III is the only land-based ICBM in service in the United States. It has a range of approximately 13,000km (8078 miles).

Glossary

air-to-air missile (AAM) A guided missile fired from an aircraft for the purpose of destroying another aircraft.

artillery Large-caliber weapons, such as cannons, howitzers, mortars, and missile launchers.

ballistic missile A missile with a high, arching trajectory that is guided in the first part of its flight but then falls freely under gravity as it approaches its target.

caliber The diameter of the barrel of a weapon; also, the diameter of the projectile used in it.

countermeasure An action taken to impair the operational effectiveness of enemy activity.

cruise missile A pilotless, jet-propelled guided missile. Cruise missiles may be armed with conventional or nuclear warheads and launched from aircraft, submarines, or land-based platforms.

howitzer A short-barreled cannon that fires explosive shells at a high angle of elevation and low velocity.

intercontinental ballistic missile (ICBM) A ballistic missile that is designed to reach a target several thousand miles away.

kiloton A measure of explosive power equal to that of 1,000 tons (1,016 tonnes) of TNT.

payload The explosive charge carried in the warhead of a missile.

projectile Object, such as a shell, that is fired from an artillery gun.

recoil The backward movement of a piece of artillery upon firing.

salvo A method of delivery in which a weapon's release mechanisms are operated to release or fire all ammunition of a specific type simultaneously.

self-propelled gun An artillery gun that is mounted on a motorized tracked or wheeled chassis and therefore does not need to be towed.

turret A self-contained structure, capable of rotation, in which weapons are mounted in a tank or other military vehicle.

warhead The part of a missile, rocket, or other munition that contains the nuclear or thermonuclear system, high explosives, chemical or biological agents, or inert materials intended to inflict damage.

For More Information

Air Force Armament Museum
100 Museum Drive
Eglin Air Force Base, FL 32542
(850) 651-1808
Web site: http://afarmamentmuseum.com
This museum features aviation warfare armament from the early days of World War I through to today's high-tech planes and bombs. Exhibits contain an extensive collection of weaponry, including many different sizes of missiles and bombs, as well as intriguing interactive displays. Vintage military aircraft are displayed outdoors.

National Museum of Nuclear Science & History
601 Eubank Boulevard SE
Albuquerque, NM 87123
(505) 245-2137
Web site: http://www.nuclearmuseum.org
At this museum, visitors can learn the story of the atomic age, from early research of nuclear development through today's peaceful uses of nuclear technology. The museum's five-acre outdoor Heritage Park features unique military objects such as rockets, missile systems, cannons, and a nuclear submarine sail.

RCA Museum: Canada's National Artillery Museum
Building N-118, Patricia Road
Shilo, MB R0K 2A0
Canada
(204) 765-3000 (ext. 3570)

Web site: http://www.rcamuseum.com
The RCA Museum presents Canadian military technology, history, and heritage. Permanent exhibits include both indoor and outdoor displays of artillery pieces, military vehicles, guns, war memorabilia, and more.

U.S. Army Artillery Museum
238 Randolph Road
Fort Sill, OK 73503
(580) 442-1819
Web site: http://sill-www.army.mil/famuseum
The U.S. Army Artillery Museum tells the story of artillery from 1775 to the present with over seventy guns and artillery pieces and numerous other artifacts, including ammunition, small arms, and uniforms.

U.S. Naval Museum of Armament and Technology
Naval Air Weapons Station, China Lake
1 Pearl Harbor Way
China Lake, CA 93555
(760) 939-3530
Web site: http://www.chinalakemuseum.org
This museum traces the heritage of one of the navy's premier weapons research, development, and testing facilities. It preserves and displays the area's unique achievements in air and surface armament and technology.

Web Sites

Due to the changing nature of Internet links, Rosen Publishing has developed an online list of Web sites related to the subject of this book. This site is updated regularly. Please use this link to access the list:

http://www.rosenlinks.com/MODW/Art

For Further Reading

Adams, Simon. *Artillery* (War Machines). Mankato, MN: Smart Apple Media in association with Imperial War Museum, 2009.
Dougherty, Martin J. *Land Warfare* (Modern Warfare). New York, NY: Gareth Stevens Publishing, 2010.
Dougherty, Martin J. *Weapons and Technology* (Modern Warfare). New York, NY: Gareth Stevens Publishing, 2010.
Fowler, Will. *The Story of Modern Weapons and Warfare* (Journey Through History). New York, NY: Rosen Central, 2012.
Fridell, Ron. *Military Technology* (Cool Science). Minneapolis, MN: Lerner Publications, 2008.
Gilpin, Daniel, and Alex Pang. *Military Vehicles* (Machines Close-Up). New York, NY: Marshall Cavendish Benchmark, 2011.
Graham, Ian. *Military Technology* (New Technology). Mankato, MN: Smart Apple Media, 2008.
Green, Michael, and Gladys Green. *Self-Propelled Howitzers: The M109A6 Paladins* (Edge Books: War Machines). Mankato, MN: Capstone Press, 2005.
Hamilton, John. *United States Army* (A & D Xtreme). Edina, MN: ABDO Publishing, 2012.
Hamilton, John. *World War II: Weapons*. Edina, MN: ABDO Publishing, 2012.
Kinard, Jeff. *Artillery: An Illustrated History of Its Impact* (Weapons and Warfare). Santa Barbara, CA: ABC-CLIO, 2007.
Loveless, Antony. *Tank Warfare* (Crabtree Contact). New York, NY: Crabtree Publishing, 2009.
Parker, Steve, and Alex Pang. *Military Machines* (How It Works). Broomall, PA: Mason Crest Publishers, 2011.
Samuels, Charlie. *Machines and Weaponry of World War I* (Machines That Won the War). New York, NY: Gareth Stevens Publishing, 2013.
Samuels, Charlie. *Machines and Weaponry of World War II* (Machines That Won the War). New York, NY: Gareth Stevens Publishing, 2013.
Shank, Carol, Margaret Griffin, and Barbara J. Fox. *U.S. Military Weapons and Artillery* (U.S. Military Technology). North Mankato, MN: Capstone Press, 2013.
Tougas, Shelley. *The Science of Weapons* (Science of War). North Mankato, MN: Compass Point Books, 2012.

Index

A

ADATS (Air Defense Anti-Tank) missile system, 22
AGM-86 CALCM (Conventional Air-Launched Cruise Missile), 24
air-defense missile launchers, 22
anti-aircraft artillery, 20
anti-tank guided weapons systems, 34
Archer, 14
artillery
    anti-aircraft, 20
    explanation of, 5
    heavy, 8
    light and medium, 7, 11
    self-propelled, 11, 13

B

B83 nuclear bomb, 40
B57 nuclear bomb, 40
bombs, 27, 28, 36, 38
Brimstone, 32
B61 nuclear bomb, 40

C

Caesar, 14
cluster munitions, 36
cruise missiles, 5, 24

D

DANA, 14

E

electromagnetic pulse (EMP), 40, 42

F

FAB, 38

G

GPS guidance systems, 5, 18, 24, 36, 38
G6, 14
gun, definition of, 5
gun vs. howitzer designation, 5, 7

H

Hellfire missile, 32
howitzer, definition of, 5
hybrid gun/missile systems, 20

I

infrared homing, 31

J

Javelin, 34

L

laser guidance, 32, 36, 38
LG-1 howitzer, 7
L118 Light Gun, 7

M

missiles, 5, 18, 20, 22, 36
    air-launched anti-tank, 32
    air-to-air, 31
    air-to-surface, 27, 28
    cruise, 5, 24
    intercontinental ballistic, 45
Mk 80 series, 27, 38
Mokopa, 32
M110, 8
mortar, definition of, 5
M777, 7

N

Nimrod, 32
nuclear bombs/explosions, 40, 42, 45

O

OTO Melara 105, 7
"over the shoulder launch," 31

P

Palmaria, 8
Primus 155mm, 8

R

radar, 24, 31, 32
rocket artillery systems
    long-range, 18
    short- to medium-range, 16

S

self-propelled guns, 11, 13
    wheeled, 14
"shoot and scoot" tactics, 13
Spike, 34

T

tandem warheads, 34
terrain-matching, 24
theater ballistic missiles, 45
tracked vehicles, 13, 14
2S4 Tyulpan, 8
2S7 Pion, 8
"tube" artillery, 5, 16

W

weapons dispensers, 36

About the Author

Martin J. Dougherty is a writer and editor specializing in military and defense topics. He is an expert on asymmetric and nonconventional warfare. His published works deal with subjects ranging from naval weapons to personal security. He is author of *Small Arms Visual Encyclopedia*, *Tanks of World War II*, and *Essential Weapons Identification Guide: Small Arms: 1945–Present*.